1991

AMERICAN HOMELESSNESS

A Reference Handbook

AMERICAN HOMELESSNESS

A Reference Handbook

Mary Ellen Hombs
National Coalition for the Homeless

CONTEMPORARY WORLD ISSUES

ABC-CLIO
Santa Barbara, California
Oxford, England

Library of Congress Cataloging-in-Publication Data

Hombs, Mary Ellen.
    American homelessness : a reference handbook / Mary Ellen Hombs.
      p. cm. — (Contemporary world issues)
    Includes bibliographical references.
    1. Homelessness—United States—Handbooks, manuals, etc.
  I. Title. II. Series.
  HV4505.H647 1990   362.5'0973—dc20   90-30936

ISBN 0-87436-547-3 (alk. paper)

97 96 95 94 93 92 91 90   10 9 8 7 6 5 4 3 2 1

ABC-CLIO, Inc.
130 Cremona Drive, P.O. Box 1911
Santa Barbara, California 93116-1911

Clio Press Ltd.
55 St. Thomas' Street
Oxford, OX1 1JG, England

This book is Smyth-sewn and printed on acid-free paper ∞ .
Manufactured in the United States of America.

To David

Contents

Preface

THE PROBLEM OF HOMELESSNESS in our nation has grown dramatically during the last decade; it now reaches into every kind of community: urban and suburban, small cities, rural areas. As a result, students at every level, their teachers, writers, and the concerned public have sought further information about the causes of homelessness and its solutions. Countless school papers and research projects have been undertaken.

For most people, the chief vehicle for understanding the causes and characteristics of homelessness has been the mass media. Yet, by their very nature, television news programs, weekly magazines, movies, and other outlets can give only the most brief and superficial exposure of significant social problems. They cannot begin to offer solutions to a problem that is complicated by many national factors: the housing market, the labor economy, national mental health policies.

There have not been any significant information sources available to assist researchers doing other than scientific studies. No comprehensive source has offered an organized overview of the wide variety of existing resources and tools for addressing the problem. As a result, researchers have frequently turned to those with the most exposure to the problem—local direct service providers—who unfortunately are also least able to spare the time to assist individuals by pointing out worthwhile information sources and may even be too hard pressed to stay abreast of national developments.

This lack of information resources has also affected the concerned citizen who is seeking some depth of understanding about a widespread and costly human problem. Ordinary citizens, persons working in religious and voluntary organizations seeking to address the problem in their local communities, and policy-makers at all levels have sought information that was accessible and organized. Moreover, they have a real need to draw on the experiences of others, and to build on lessons already learned elsewhere.

This book represents an effort to fill that gap. In many ways, a reference book is the perfect answer to the need that exists, because it can provide a thorough introduction and overview with some economy of form. The survey of key events and players of the 1980s, for instance, provides an initial timeline of significant activity in the areas of shelter development, litigation, legislation, direct public action, and national services.

Some of these same categories of interest are used to focus on major aspects of the problem of homelessness through the presentation of documents and reports from other sources. The problem of homelessness is examined to show the influences of housing costs, lack of food, effects of mental illness, the challenge of alcohol recovery, and problems of living with HIV illness. Major efforts to reverse homelessness through litigation and federal legislation are also covered in detail.

Because homelessness is such a complex problem, there are many sorts of professional and voluntary organizations, as well as government agencies, involved in studying, addressing, and solving it. A selective listing of these groups offers sources for further pursuit of specialized interests and opportunities for personal involvement. An extensive reference bibliography, organized by topic, presents the opportunity either to research these same interests or to undertake reading that will provide a working knowledge of the problem.

Finally, a wide variety of nonprint media—including videos, films, databases, and exhibits—is available for education and research use. A glossary of common terms helps unravel some of the vocabulary encountered in studying homelessness.

My perspective on the problem of homelessness and the need for these information resources has been formed by two decades of experience at the local and national level, in the hands-on efforts of providing food and refuge for the homeless, as well as in the roles of advocate, educator, and researcher. Seventeen years of my work took place in the unique environment of the Community for Creative Non-Violence (CCNV) in Washington, D.C.; more recently, I have administered the federal and national policy and organizing work of the National Coalition for the Homeless.

It is likely that this book will make the problem of homelessness more understandable to readers; some may even admire the efforts of the individuals they read about. It is important to remember, however, that the "problem" of homelessness affects individuals: men, women, and children. The homeless are human beings: hurting, crying, bleeding, sweating, freezing human beings. Whatever understanding comes from reading this book should be applied to ending homelessness and setting aright the lives of those who experience it.

1

Introduction

DURING THE DECADE OF THE 1980s, the problem of homelessness has received increasing attention across the country; the sheer visibility of contemporary homelessness is perhaps its most identifiable attribute. Whether it is the sight of a family living in a car, or the thousands in the streets and subways of New York City, or the ragged men and women silhouetted against the monuments and memorials of the nation's capital, striking images of utmost poverty are inescapable for most Americans. In a recent poll, 51 percent of those responding said they personally see homeless people in their communities or on their commutes to work. This figure reflects a 39 percent increase over responses just three years ago.[1]

One researcher has examined several indicators of the visibility of the problem and the attention devoted to it. He found that, in 1975, no newspaper, magazine, or journal articles appeared on the subject of homelessness. However, in 1986, 48 such articles were listed in the *Reader's Guide to Periodical Literature*. Further, he found that more than 40 research studies on the homeless had appeared by 1988. In addition, during the 1987–1988 session of Congress, 32 separate bills related to homelessness were introduced.[2]

Portions of this introductory material were previously published as "Federal Policy for the Homeless" in Volume 1 of the *Stanford Law and Policy Review* of Stanford Law School (©1989 by the Board of Trustees of the Leland Stanford Junior University). They are used here by agreement with the Board of Trustees of Leland Stanford Junior University.

From coast to coast, communities of all sizes have discovered within their own borders a new version of a problem many previously associated only with the Depression years in the United States, or only with a certain individual stereotype. Yet the images of the evening news and the ragged individual behaving bizarrely on a downtown street corner are not the figures either of the Depression and Dustbowl years or, more recently, of the 1950s and 1960s, when the common idea of a homeless person was a middle-aged, white, male alcoholic who was no doubt homeless by choice. These current images describe a new version of the problem, one that involves families with children, runaway youth, and homeless adults.

So, while homelessness itself is not new, what is new is the size and scope of the problem, how it has come about, who it affects, and what our individual and collective attitudes are toward it. In the last decade, homelessness has reached epidemic proportions in this country. As the number of those affected continues to increase, service providers and public officials alike recognize that the problem is complex, touching on many issues of poverty, public assistance levels, disability, affordable housing, and more.

The nation faces a significant challenge: Not only do people continue to be pushed into the streets, but for some escape from the streets seems nearly impossible. At the end of the 1980s, research shows that homelessness continues to grow around the nation—in large communities and small—and families with children continue to represent the most rapidly expanding segment of the homeless population.[3]

This book offers resources for further reference and research into homelessness in the United States in the 1980s. This introductory essay offers an overview of the structure of the problem.

What Does It Mean To Be Homeless?

What are we talking about when we talk about homelessness? Are homeless people just those we see sleeping outside on the streets, panhandling, sleeping in front of national monuments? What about people in emergency shelters? What if an individual has a nearby relative and chooses not to stay with that person? Is someone homeless when friends or family offer temporary accommodations on a sofa? Do we really mean that someone is "houseless" when we talk about this problem, or does homelessness mean more than the mere absence of shelter?

Unfortunately, there is no single, generally accepted definition of homelessness, although clearly the choice of a definition has significant impact when estimating the size of the problem of homelessness. Various agencies of the federal government have even used several different definitions during the last decade. Among the major definitions are:

A person is homeless if his or her residence at night is "(a) in public or private emergency shelters which take a variety of forms—armories, schools, church basements, government buildings, former firehouses and, where temporary vouchers are provided by private or public agencies, even hotels, apartments, or boarding homes; or (b) in the streets, parks, subways, bus terminals, railroad stations, airports, under bridges or aqueducts, abandoned buildings without utilities, cars, trucks, or any other public or private space that is not designed for shelter."[4] This definition, it should be noted, does not include people in halfway houses or long-term detoxification residences; it does not include incarcerated persons who would otherwise be in shelters or on the streets. It does, however, include battered women, if they are on the streets or in a shelter or group house.

A homeless person is "anyone who lacks adequate shelter, resources, and community ties."[5]

A homeless individual (1) lacks a fixed, regular, and adequate nighttime residence and (2) has a primary nighttime residence that is (a) a supervised, publicly or privately operated shelter designed to provide temporary living accommodations (including welfare hotels, congregate shelters, and transitional housing for the mentally ill), (b) an institution that provides a temporary residence for individuals intended to be institutionalized, or (c) a public or private place not designed for, or ordinarily used as, a regular sleeping accommodation for human beings.[6]

Persons who are living "doubled up" with friends or family in precarious, makeshift housing arrangements lack the "fixed, regular, and adequate nighttime residence" described above and should be considered homeless;[7] they are some of the people included in the description "hidden homeless."

While not seeking to define homelessness, the U.S. Bureau of the Census combined two categories of "transient" persons in its 1980 census and plans to do so in the 1990 count. It will count "(a) all persons at missions, flophouses, and other transient accommodations renting for less than $4 per night; local jails and similar short-term detention centers; and places such as all-night theaters, railroad stations, and bus depots"; as well as "(b) transient persons (i.e., 'street people') missed in all other housing units and found on street corners, bus and train stations, welfare offices, food stamp centers, and so on."[8]

"But being homeless means more than not having a place to sleep. Being homeless means having no place to save the things that connect you to your past, losing all contact with friends and family, uprooting your children from school. It means suffering the frustration and degradation of living hand to mouth, depending on the generosity of strangers or the efficiency of a government agency for your survival, for your children's survival."[9]

Who Is Homeless?

At the beginning of the decade, the prevailing stereotype of a homeless person was that of a middle-aged, white, urban, male alcoholic, a transient who either wandered the country (as a "vagrant," "tramp," or "hobo") or inhabited downtown "skid row" areas characterized by low-cost hotels and bars. Most of all, this person was viewed as "shiftless" for not living a "responsible" life with job and family and as blameworthy for whatever poverty, misery, or suffering accompanied this voluntarily chosen lifestyle. Traditionally, the only services available to this homeless person were church services, those of the "mission" establishments such as the Salvation Army and the Gospel Mission, which offered overnight sleeping space and meals in exchange for a fee and a sincere desire to rehabilitate one's life by attending mandatory sermons and renouncing alcohol. In proportion to the numbers who might seek this path to help, few of the available beds were for homeless women. No longer does this description of the homeless hold true. As the causes of homelessness have broadened and become more tied to fundamental economic changes in our nation, homelessness has become both a symptom of more chronic poverty and an event that can cut across traditional defenses of income, education, or geography. The population of the streets has been democratized correspondingly. Recent studies of the homeless have found these trends:

1. More and more, the homeless are young people; estimates center around 25 percent.[10]
2. Minority groups are disproportionately represented.[11]
3. Families with children constitute approximately 35 percent of the homeless.[12]
4. In most areas, working people account for an average of 30 percent of the homeless population.[13]
5. More and more, homelessness is found to be a chronic and recurring event.[14]

Not only families are homeless. Single adults are, too, often because they have suffered a job loss, trouble at home, or a health problem. Veterans are discharged from the military; prisoners are released after serving sentences; young adults "graduate" from the foster care system. Any of these people could become homeless.

Significant minorities of the homeless are mentally ill (30 percent),[15] are alcohol or drug dependent, or have AIDS.[16]

Literal homelessness, however, is only the most extreme manifestation of a more general, growing, and enduring poverty caused in part by drastic cuts in federal low-income housing programs and exacerbated by a combination of other factors and personal difficulties: rising housing costs, related safety-net programs cuts, and a minimum wage that has not been increased since 1981, for example.

And for each individual or household that actually reaches the streets or shelters, many more are living on the edge of homelessness, doubled- or tripled-up in precarious housing arrangements with friends or family, a phenomenon that increased from 15 percent of poor households in 1978 to 28 percent of the poor in 1985.[17] The 1985 American Housing Survey estimated that more than 1 million households live in overcrowded conditions, one substantial indicator of the housing crisis.[18] Further, in some markets, people resort to living in structures not intended to be used as housing—garages, for example.[19]

How Many People Are Homeless?

From the difficulty revealed in arriving at a definition of homelessness, it should be apparent that there is also no adequate way to arrive at an estimate of the size of the homeless population. There has been enormous controversy over this point since the problem began to burgeon in the early 1980s—just as the economy was on an upswing—and advocates, researchers, and government officials remain greatly divided over estimates. Figures have been offered publicly ranging from a low of 250,000 people to at least 3 million.[20]

Substantial problems of methodology exist in trying to count homeless people, not the least of which is that many homeless people work very hard to obscure their homelessness by dress, appearance, and daily schedule. They try to make their homelessness invisible to those who might not otherwise recognize it. Still others achieve their invisibility by sleeping in abandoned buildings, in cars parked behind shopping malls, or in tents in the woods. And, as revealed by the definitional problem, the homelessness of many others is hidden by their apparently being housed in precarious arrangements with friends or families, circumstances that can be ended in a moment. As previously pointed out, still others make do in structures not intended as living quarters. No disagreement is apparent, however, over the question of a growing problem.

What Causes Homelessness?

Several major contributing causes have been identified by those examining the growth of homelessness.

Deinstitutionalization

While widely viewed as the primary cause of homelessness in the early 1980s, deinstitutionalization itself was not to blame. The theory of releasing mental patients from long-term hospital care when they did not require such a setting was a good one. What resulted, however, was careless depopulation of state institutions, without the necessary community support facilities and services that would allow previous patients to live securely in the community. When deinstitutionalization combined with tightened readmission standards at the same hospitals, the wave of vulnerable dischargees was, as characterized by one psychiatrist, "dumped amid the broken promises."[21]

As previously stated, general agreement exists as to the national prevalence of serious mental illness, including schizophrenia and manic depression, among the homeless. Experts state that there are twice as many homeless mentally ill persons as there are institutionalized patients, as well as increasing numbers of incarcerated people with mental illness, many of whom were homeless when jailed and will be homeless upon their release.[22] As long as there is little provision for released patients and inadequate housing available in the community, the plight of the homeless mentally ill will be dismal.[23]

Increasing Poverty and Decreasing Assistance

The economic recovery of the early 1980s did not reach everyone in the nation; the homeless and those at risk ended the decade in worse shape than before. Today, in the richest country in the world, 13.5 percent of all Americans are poor.[24] Some 32.5 million people are living below the officially defined poverty level.[25] Over a ten-year period, 25 percent of all Americans will slip into poverty at one time or another.[26] Those hit hardest by poverty are children and youth: children under 18 are 40 percent of those in poverty.[27]

The 1987 poverty rate for white Americans was 10.5 percent, representing a very slight drop from the previous 11 percent rate.[28] But the rate was 33.1 percent for African-Americans and 28.2 percent for Hispanics, and both African-American and Hispanic poverty have been increasing.[29]

Inequalities in income distribution in this country have reached their greatest extreme—for both rich and poor households—for the entire period in which such data have been collected.[30] The most wealthy 20 percent of the population received the highest percentage of income ever recorded (43.7 percent), while the poorest 40 percent received 15.4 percent, the lowest ever recorded.[31]

Clearly, the rich got richer and the poor got poorer: The poverty gap—the amount by which poor people's income fell below the poverty line—*widened* and, despite general economic recovery, the poverty rate failed to drop significantly. According to one report, 81 percent of urban mayors felt the economic recovery did not benefit their city's hungry, homeless, or poor.[32]

While the numbers of the poor increase and their economic position in society worsens, qualitative changes in their ranks suggest the problem may be more widespread than in the past. The face of poverty increasingly reveals victims who are minorities, women who are heads of households, and younger married couples. These groups are not the temporary poor likely to be well served by emergency measures in either the public or private sector. Instead they include victims of lingering racial discrimination and sexism, people educationally unprepared for the vast structural changes in the nation's economy and people often trapped in decaying inner-city environments where all their available energies are sapped by the struggle to survive.

The Working Poor

Increasingly, the ranks of the homeless poor include working people, because housing costs are rising beyond the reach of low wages. According to one report, 56 percent of mayors blamed low wages and rising housing costs as a primary employment-related cause of homelessness.[33] The minimum wage has remained unchanged since 1981, while inflation has increased by 31 percent. More than 75 percent of the new jobs in the economy in the past decade have been minimum-wage jobs.[34] When this is coupled with the rising costs of housing, it is not difficult to see why many shelters are populated with workers who have nowhere else to live. Estimates of the working homeless average 22 percent in many areas[35] and range as high as 83 percent in some.[36]

Cuts in Safety-Net Programs

The benefits programs that once would have constituted a final protection from the streets have been greatly eroded. Programs designed to help people out of poverty or ease the misery it causes have been cut or have failed to keep up with the cost of living. Cuts often occur in the form of tightened eligibility standards. Ironically, the very fact of being homeless—having no fixed address, being subject to robbery and weather, being unable to keep appointments—can make it impossible to establish benefits to which the homeless person is legitimately entitled. Program cuts have disproportionately affected minorities.[37] From 1970 to 1988, the average value of Aid to Families with Dependent Children (AFDC) benefits, which provide federal aid to poor children, fell 35 percent to only 44.2 percent of the federal poverty level.[38] In more than two-thirds of cities surveyed around the country, inadequate welfare benefits are seen as contributing to homelessness.[39]

The Shortage of Affordable Housing

The influence that income problems have on the search for housing is very real, for it is the critical shortage of low-cost housing that makes the difference between chronic hardship and outright homelessness.[40] A recent MIT study put the 1983 shortfall of dwelling units available at $250 or less per month at 3 million units and rapidly growing, with a forecast of 18.7 million people in need of affordable housing in 2003.[41] The Low Income Housing Information Service (LIHIS) estimates there are about twice as many very low income families seeking housing as there are available affordable units, with the number of very low income renter households exceeding the number of units by a national average of 93.7 percent.[42]

The Federal Role

The 1980s have witnessed a radical reversal of the federal government's 40-year commitment to providing low-income housing, with the dire consequence that assisted housing availability does not nearly meet demand. According to one report, 84 percent of the cities surveyed reported an average 26 percent increase in the demand for assisted housing in 1987.[43]

Throughout his administration, President Ronald Reagan firmly stated his views on the appropriate federal role in providing direct aid for the homeless and ill-housed. On July 22, 1987, he reluctantly signed the landmark Stewart B. McKinney Homeless Assistance Act into law. According to the White House, the president put his signature on the McKinney Act in the evening in order to demonstrate his "lack of enthusiasm" for the measure.[44]

As he left office, former president Reagan reiterated the personal views on homelessness that constituted the approach of the previous eight years: that the homeless are on the streets by choice and prefer this to the available shelters, that "a large proportion" of them have mental problems, and that the jobless are simply not motivated.[45] Nevertheless, in a 1989 poll, 65 percent of those responding favored greater federal spending on homelessness.[46]

Under President Reagan and his housing and urban development secretary, Samuel Pierce (the only Cabinet officer to serve eight years under Reagan), the budget for federal low-income housing programs plummeted drastically from 1981–1988; the budget authority for low-income housing programs fell from over $30 billion in 1981 to a proposed fiscal year 1990 (FY 90) figure of $6.7 billion.

Even so, these were smaller cuts than originally requested by the Reagan administration. Some 700,000 subsidized units came into existence despite the ceiling the administration desired, though planned or occupied units would have numbered an additional 1.7 million if FY 81 spending levels had continued.[47] Public housing construction alone dropped from 30,000 units in 1982 to about 2,200 in 1987.[48] An estimated 1 million people are on waiting lists for public housing.[49]

Further, the demand for assisted housing will only rise in the foreseeable future, as more than 1.9 million federally subsidized units in privately owned buildings stand to be lost to the low-income market through mortgage prepayments and expiring subsidy contracts coming up through the year 2005.[50] Hundreds of thousands of low-income people face displacement through this process, which has already begun. The U.S. Department of Housing and Urban Development (HUD) estimates that the number of units that might be lost by 1996 is 470,000–577,000; the Government Accounting Office (GAO) prediction is 900,000 units.[51]

The Private Market

Unsubsidized, low-rent housing in the private sector is also in crisis. The number of units available at rents of $250 per month or less in 1974 was 11 million, with about 9 million households constituting the demand. By 1983, these proportions had reversed themselves: The stock numbered only about 9 million units, with about 12 million households in need. While about 20 million units were added to the housing stock during this period, only 1 million assisted units—created mostly through Section 8—were "affordable."[52] From 1970 to 1982, many cities lost from 50–85 percent of their single room occupancy (SRO) rooms.[53] The General Accounting Office (GAO) estimated that 1.1 million SRO units were lost during this time period.[54] Such hotels are a traditional source of low-cost housing for single people.

The Response to Homelessness

As the problem of homelessness has grown nationally, and as the federal housing budget has been cut, various sectors of society have responded. Volunteer efforts offering food, shelter, and other services have expanded dramatically, with both religious and civic groups playing a role. State and local governments have sometimes helped provide shelter and services. Foundations and religious organizations have addressed the serious health care needs of those who live outside in all kinds of weather without adequate protection. Some individuals and organizations with access to the media have helped raise the visibility of the problem, through routes as diverse as cartoons and television movies. Books have been written and newspaper articles published. Dramatic public events such as funerals and memorials have brought the grim reality of suffering to television news.

Demonstrations have brought citizens to the doorstep of even the White House to demand assistance for those in need. Community nonprofit organizations, along with state and local governments, and even business, have tried in some areas to meet the growing demand for affordable housing. Renovation of old buildings, creation of new units, and adaptation of other facilities have been undertaken as people seek to answer the need of those around them.

The following chapters offer resources for further research into both past and existing programs as well as future possibilities for alleviating this very complex and painful problem.

Notes

1. Robin Toner, "Homeless Gaining Wider Visibility," *New York Times,* 22 January 1989, A-1.

2. Peter Rossi, *Without Shelter: Homelessness in the 1980s* (New York: Priority Press Publications, 1989), 3.

3. For a description of how homelessness continues to increase around the nation, see National Coalition for the Homeless, *American Nightmare: A Decade of Homelessness in the United States* (Washington, DC: National Coalition for the Homeless, 1989).

4. Department of Housing and Urban Development (HUD), *A Report to the Secretary on the Homeless and Emergency Shelters,* May 1984, 7–8.

5. Irene Shifren Levine, "Homelessness: Its Implications for Mental Health Policy and Practice," prepared for the Annual Meeting of the American Psychological Association, August 30, 1983, 1.

6. Stewart B. McKinney Homeless Assistance Act (PL 100-77).

7. U.S. General Accounting Office (GAO), *Homeless Children and Youth: About 68,000 Homeless and 186,000 in Shared Housing at Any Given Time* (Washington, DC: U.S. GAO, June 1989), 8.

8. Statement of William Hill, April 1986, Regional Director, New York Regional Office, Field Division, Bureau of the Census, before the Subcommittee on Census and Population, New York City.

9. National Coalition for the Homeless, *Homelessness in America: A Summary* (New York: National Coalition for the Homeless, 1989), 1.

10. National Coalition, *American Nightmare*.

11. Ibid.

12. Ibid.

13. Ibid.

14. Michael R. Sosin, Paul Colson, Susan Grossman, School of Social Work Administration, University of Chicago, *Homelessness in Chicago: Poverty and Pathology, Social Institutions and Social Change* (Chicago: Chicago Community Trust, 1988), 262.

15. E. Fuller Torrey, M.D., *Nowhere To Go: The Tragic Odyssey of the Homeless Mentally Ill* (New York: Harper & Row, 1988), 7.

16. National Coalition, *American Nightmare*.

17. Paul A. Leonard, Cushing N. Dolbeare, and Edward B. Lazere, *A Place to Call Home: The Crisis in Housing for the Poor* (Washington, DC: Center on Budget and Policy Priorities and Low Income Housing Information Service, 1989), 24.

18. Ibid., 23.

19. A *Los Angeles Times* survey in 1987 estimated that 42,288 families were living in garages in Los Angeles County. There were an average of five members in these families, according to the survey, resulting in an estimate of 148,500 children living in garages. Reported in U.S. General Accounting Office, *Homeless Children and Youth* (Washington, DC: U.S. GAO, 1989), 16.

20. The 250,000 figure was first asserted in the 1984 study released by the U.S. Department of Housing and Urban Development. The current assistant secretary of community planning and development, S. Anna Kondratas, was one of the chief public defenders of this figure, which was criticized as low by advocates. In September 1989, however, Kondratas stated during her Senate confirmation hearings that she endorsed the 650,000 figure offered in the National Academy of Science's 1988 report *Homelessness, Health and Human Needs*. Advocacy organizations, however, believe at least 3 million people are homeless. Among these groups are the Community for Creative Non-Violence, which first announced this figure in 1982, and the National Coalition for the Homeless.

21. Torrey, *Nowhere To Go*, 3.

22. Ibid., 5.

23. Ibid.

24. Martin Tolchin, "Minority Poverty on Rise but White Poor Decline," *New York Times*, 1 September 1988.

25. Center on Budget and Policy Priorities, *Poverty Remains High Despite Economic Recovery* (Washington, DC: Center on Budget and Policy Priorities, 1988).

26. Center on Budget and Policy Priorities, *Smaller Slices of the Pie: The Grow-

ing Economic Vulnerability of Poor and Moderate Income Americans (Washington, DC: Center on Budget and Policy Priorities, 1985), 17.

27. Tolchin, *New York Times.*

28. Center on Budget and Policy Priorities, *Poverty Remains High.*

29. Tolchin, *New York Times.*

30. Center on Budget and Policy Priorities, *Poverty Remains High.*

31. Tolchin, *New York Times.*

32. U.S. Conference of Mayors, *The Continuing Growth of Hunger, Homelessness and Poverty in America's Cities: 1987. A 26-City Survey* (Washington, DC: U.S. Conference of Mayors, January 1987), 58.

33. Ibid., 26.

34. Ibid., 87.

35. Ibid., 22.

36. Mary Jordan, "In '87, 83% in N. Va. Shelters Were Employed, Study Says," *Washington Post,* 19 August 1988.

37. Center on Budget and Policy Priorities, *Still Far from the Dream* (Washington, DC: Center on Budget and Policy Priorities, 1988), 41.

38. Committee on Ways and Means, U.S. House of Representatives, *Background Material and Data on Programs within the Jurisdiction of the Committee on Ways and Means,* 1988 edition, 415.

39. U.S. Conference of Mayors, *A Status Report on Homeless Families in America's Cities* (Washington, DC: U.S. Conference of Mayors, 1987), 21.

40. This section utilizes a "moderate income" standard of less than 80 percent of median income in a given area, and a "low income" standard of less than 50 percent of median income. "Affordable housing" is therefore defined as being available to these households at 30 percent of their income.

41. Phillip Clay, *At Risk of Loss: The Endangered Future of Low-Income Rental Housing Resources* (Cambridge, MA: MIT, 1987), 4, 24.

42. Isaac Shapiro and Robert Greenstein, *Holes in the Safety Net: Poverty Programs and Policies in the States—National Overview* (Washington, DC: Center on Budget and Policy Priorities, 1988), 48.

43. Conference of Mayors, *Growth of Hunger,* 43.

44. Robert Pear, "President Signs $1 Billion Bill in Homeless Aid," *New York Times,* 24 July 1987, A1.

45. Steven V. Roberts, "Reagan on Homelessness: Many Choose to Live in the Streets," *New York Times,* 22 December 1988.

46. Toner, *New York Times.*

47. Cushing N. Dolbeare, *Background Data on Low Income Housing* (Washington, DC: Low Income Housing Information Service, 1988), 1.

48. Council of Large Public Housing Authorities (CLPHA), *Public Housing Tomorrow* (Washington, DC: Council of Large Public Housing Authorities,

1988), 7.

49. Michael Stegman, "Maximizing a Social Investment: The Increasing Value of Public Housing," *CRIT 20*, The Architectural Student Journal, Spring 1988, 10.

50. Clay, *At Risk of Loss*, 7.

51. David C. Schwartz, Richard C. Ferlauto, and Daniel N. Hoffman, *A New Housing Policy: Recapturing the American Dream* (Philadelphia: Temple University Press, 1988), 24.

52. Clay, *At Risk of Loss*, 4.

53. Schwartz, *A New Housing Policy*, 204.

54. Ibid., 23.

2

Chronology

THE FOLLOWING IS A SELECTED CHRONOLOGY of events concerning advocacy for the homeless. The early developments of the decade reflect the efforts of advocates seeking to address local problems that were not yet viewed as precursors of a coming crisis. As homelessness grew in visibility and scope, so did significant responses to it, with events becoming more numerous and reflecting a national network of action. By the close of the 1980s, the general public was seeking solutions from the highest levels of government.

1976   Community for Creative Non-Violence (CCNV) begins campaign to offer shelter to all who need it in Washington, D.C.

1978   CCNV starts two-week occupation of the National Visitors Center (Union Station) as a shelter for the homeless in Washington, D.C., to dramatize the number of homeless people in the city.

1979   *Callahan v. Carey* lawsuit filed in New York City by volunteer Wall Street attorney Robert M. Hayes to establish a right to shelter for homeless men.

1980   CCNV burns census forms to protest inadequate measures for counting the homeless in the 1980 national census.

        Williams v. Barry lawsuit filed in Washington, D.C., to prevent closing of city-run shelters for men with only 48 hours' notice.

1980
cont.
Coalition for the Homeless formed in New York City as a result of public activities in response to removal of homeless people from the area around Madison Square Garden, site of the Democratic National Convention.

"A Forced March to Nowhere," an initial CCNV survey of homelessness and services around the nation, presented to House District Committee hearing on urban problems.

1981
Demonstrators block Pennsylvania Avenue to protest reduced provisions for the poor announced in the first Reagan administration budget the previous evening.

Private Lives/Public Spaces: Homeless Adults on the Streets of New York City released after researchers Kim Hopper and Ellen Baxter completed a lengthy and groundbreaking survey of homeless people in that city.

"Call to Prayer" begins at White House: six weeks of daily demonstrations protesting the impact of the Reagan budget on the poor.

Consent decree signed in *Callahan v. Carey* lawsuit, providing overnight shelter for single homeless men in New York City, as well as court-ordered standards for the operation and expansion of shelters for men.

The Long Loneliness in Baltimore, a survey of homelessness in Baltimore, released.

Massachusetts Coalition for the Homeless formed.

Building commences on "Reaganville" demonstration tent encampment in Lafayette Park across from the White House, by members of CCNV, who served a traditional Thanksgiving meal in the park. Protest was to recall the "Hooverville" homeless settlements of the Depression. Demonstrators were arrested, but tents remained until spring.

Memorial service for the nation's homeless in Lafayette Park, across from the White House. Service attended by hundreds of advocates from around the country, who plant more than 400 crosses bearing names and dates of death for homeless people.

1982
Eldredge v. Koch filed in New York City to extend right to shelter to homeless women.

1982
cont.
Homeless advocates remove crosses for the homeless dead from Lafayette Park, where they were planted during memorial service in December 1981. Advocates carry the crosses to Capitol Hill and present one to each member of Congress.

National Coalition for the Homeless formed.

Klosterman v. Carey filed, seeking housing for former state psychiatric patients who are homeless.

Luncheon for members of Congress to highlight use of salvaged food and level of food waste in the nation. The entire meal prepared by CCNV from useable food salvaged from dumpsters, including quiche, raspberry tarts, and crab.

Central City Shelter Network formed in San Francisco.

The Homeless of Phoenix: A Profile, an initial effort at studying the city's growing homeless population, released.

Consortium for the Homeless formed in Phoenix.

Homeless Caucus formed in San Francisco.

Koster v. Webb filed in Long Island's Nassau County as a federal challenge to poor shelter conditions for homeless families.

Homelessness in America: A Forced March to Nowhere, by Mary Ellen Hombs and Mitch Snyder, released as national survey of homelessness and responses to it in cities around the nation, as well as an examination of Reagan administration policies. The book is released in conjunction with congressional hearings held the same day.

"Homelessness in America," the first congressional hearings on the homeless since the Depression, convened by the Housing Subcommittee led by Representative Henry B. Gonzalez (D-TX).

Homeless people, shelter providers, and elected officials from around the nation testify on the growing problem of homelessness.

1983
People's State of the Union Address: 163 homeless people, shelter providers, civil rights and peace movement leaders arrested for occupying the Capitol rotunda, demanding food, shelter, and jobs for the poor.

1983
cont. The Emergency Jobs Appropriations Act of 1983 passes in Congress, providing $100 million for emergency food and shelter.

Soup line held in U.S. Capitol to protest the shortage of resources for the hungry and homeless.

Thirty-day fast and encampment seeking release of additional surplus food begins in Kansas City, site of the largest of the government-operated storage facilities for surplus commodities.

Campaign for the right to overnight shelter begins in Washington, D.C.; goal is a ballot initiative on the November 1984 presidential ballot.

First organizational meeting of National Coalition for the Homeless.

Homelessness in Chicago, an initial study of homeless people in that city, released.

Hodge v. Ginsberg filed; will become a successful West Virginia case to establish a right to shelter.

Formation of Committee for Freedom and Dignity in Philadelphia.

More than Shelter: A Community Response to Homelessness, a city-sponsored survey of homelessness, released in Boston.

Eisenheim v. Board of Supervisors, an early case to establish access to emergency shelter without extensive documentation, filed in Los Angeles.

1984 Federal City College shelter opens for men at the site of the old Securities and Exchange Commission building in downtown Washington, D.C.

Second congressional hearings on homelessness in the United States held in basement of homeless shelter operated by CCNV.

Maticka v. Atlantic City lawsuit filed in New Jersey to establish a right to shelter.

Arguments heard in U.S. Supreme Court in "Reaganville" case of *CCNV v. Clark,* an attempt to establish the right of homeless people to demonstrate by sleeping in Lafayette Park, across from the White House.

1984
cont.
Homeless people and shelter providers and advocates march on the White House to mark the last-minute extension of an agreement by the U.S. Department of Health and Human Services to continue use of the only federal building being used as an emergency shelter—the old Federal City College building operated by CCNV.

Congressional hearing on HUD report on homelessness. Report is widely criticized by advocates for assertion that only 250,000 people are homeless.

U.S. Supreme Court rules in *CCNV v. Clark* case stemming from 1981 encampment in Lafayette Park. The court rules against the right of homeless people to demonstrate by sleeping in the park.

Eleven homeless people and CCNV shelter providers, including Mitch Snyder, fast to secure the rehabilitation of shelter housed in the Federal City College in Washington, D.C. Five fast on water only; fast ends November 4, 1984, two days before the presidential election, when President Ronald Reagan agrees to renovate the building into a model shelter.

Initiative 17, the "D.C. Right to Overnight Shelter" law, passes, receiving support from 72 percent of the city's voters.

1985
Second organizational meeting of the National Coalition for the Homeless.

1986
"Hands Across America"—millions of Americans join hands to form a human chain across the country to raise funds for the hungry and homeless.

Third and final fast begins to secure CCNV shelter.

Mitch Snyder and homeless advocate Michael Stoops of Portland, Oregon, move to the east side of the U.S. Capitol grounds to live while they work for passage of $500 million legislation to aid the homeless.

1987
HR 558, Urgent Relief for the Homeless, is introduced by the House leadership.

"Voices from the Streets," a drama by and about homeless people, is presented at the Capitol on the evening prior to the first vote on HR 558.

1987
cont.   HR 558, now the Stewart B. McKinney Homeless Assistance Act, is signed by President Reagan.

1988   *Mixon v. Grinker* filed in New York City to seek "medically appropriate" housing for homeless people infected with the HIV virus.

Ten thousand homeless people, their supporters, and civil rights leaders march in Atlanta just prior to the "Super Tuesday" presidential primaries.

Grand opening of newly renovated Federal City Shelter, operated by CCNV in Washington, D.C., as comprehensive service model.

Daily protests demanding congressional action to house the homeless occur at the U.S. Capitol, while fasters hold vigil on the Capitol steps, calling for more housing for the poor.

Ten thousand march in New York City for action to house the homeless.

1989   Two hundred homeless people and activists meet for two days in Atlanta to form a national agenda to end homelessness and provide affordable housing.

President George Bush calls for full funding of the McKinney homeless assistance programs in his first budget message to Congress.

Palmieri v. Cuomo filed in New York State seeking residential drug treatment on demand for homeless addicts.

Housing Now!, a historic and broad-based coalition to end homelessness and secure affordable housing, brings hundreds of thousands of marchers to Washington, D.C.

3

Biographical Sketches

A VARIETY OF DIFFERENT PEOPLE have been involved in the issue of homelessness as it has become visible during the 1980s. These individuals represent a wide range of professions—including academic research, medicine, and the law—as well as the homeless themselves and their advocates. The following sketches offer an overview of those who have been prominent.

Richard Appelbaum

Currently associate professor of sociology at the University of California at Santa Barbara, Richard Appelbaum holds a Ph.D. from the University of Chicago. Appelbaum has written numerous books and articles on housing; he has been involved in a number of large-scale survey research projects. He was the chief witness to discredit the methodology of the May 1984 U.S. Department of Housing and Urban Development (HUD) report before Congress. He is a member of the national task force on housing policy associated with the Institute for Policy Studies.

Ellen Bassuk

Ellen Bassuk, M.D., is president of The Better Homes Foundation, established in 1988 in Newton, Massachusetts. She is associate professor of psychiatry at Harvard Medical School and is an expert on psychiatric emergency care and related policy issues, such as deinstitutionalization. Since 1982, Bassuk has conducted clinical research projects on the needs of the homeless mentally ill and mothers and children.

Ellen Baxter

Ellen Baxter is director of The Heights, a model single room occupancy (SRO) project for the homeless in the Washington Heights neighborhood of Manhattan. She holds a master's degree in public health from Columbia University. With Kim Hopper, she wrote the groundbreaking study *Private Lives/Public Spaces,* about the homeless in New York City, while she was a researcher at the Community Service Society.

Robert Callahan

Robert Callahan was 53 in 1979 when he became the named plaintiff in the landmark right-to-shelter suit, *Callahan v. Carey,* in New York City. Callahan was a former short order cook who became homeless for the first time at age 49 but was scared away from the existing Men's Shelter when he went there for help. He met attorney Robert Hayes at the Holy Name Center for Homeless Men, a Catholic day center on the Bowery, and agreed to be part of the suit.

Cushing Dolbeare

A consultant on housing and public policy, Cushing Dolbeare founded and is former executive director of the National Low Income Housing Coalition and the Low Income Housing Information Service. She was previously executive secretary of the National Rural Housing Coalition, managing director of the Housing Association of Delaware Valley, and associate director of the Citizens Planning and Housing Association of Baltimore. A member of the board of directors of the National Coalition for the Homeless, Dolbeare has written extensively on national housing policy.

Henry B. Gonzalez

Representative Henry B. Gonzalez was first elected to the U.S. House of Representatives in 1961; he represents the 20th Congressional District in San Antonio, Texas. He currently chairs the Banking, Finance, and Urban Affairs Committee of the House, and has chaired its Housing and Community Development Subcommittee since 1981. In 1982, he chaired the first congressional hearings since the Great Depression on homelessness and has subsequently convened dozens of other hearings on related issues.

Chester Hartman

Chester Hartman holds a Ph.D. in city and regional planning from Harvard University. He has been active in community housing and neighborhood struggles and has taught at Harvard, Yale, Cornell, the University of North Carolina, and UC Berkeley. He chairs the Planners Network and is a Fellow at the Institute for Policy Studies in Washington, D.C. He is the author of numerous books on housing policy and has been a consultant to numerous federal, state, and local government agencies. He was an expert witness at the congressional hearings on the May 1984 HUD report.

Robert M. Hayes

Robert M. Hayes filed the landmark New York City right-to-shelter case, *Callahan v. Carey*, in 1979, while an attorney at the Wall Street firm of Sullivan and Cromwell. He left the firm in 1982 and founded both the Coalition for the Homeless, oriented to New York City issues, and the National Coalition for the Homeless. Hayes also filed or assisted numerous other homelessness-related legal actions and remains associated with the organizations he started. He joined the law firm of O'Melveny and Myers in October 1989.

Kim Hopper

Kim Hopper is an assistant professor of anthropology at the New School for Social Research in New York City. He holds a Ph.D. in sociomedical science from Columbia University. He was previously a research associate at the Community Service Society, where he coauthored with Ellen Baxter the landmark study *Private Lives/Public Spaces*. He was a founder and has been a member of the board of directors of the New York City Coalition for the Homeless and the National Coalition for the Homeless. He is the author of numerous monographs and articles and has been an expert witness in many civil suits concerning the rights and needs of the homeless.

Jim Hubbard

Jim Hubbard is a photographer who directs "Shooting Back," a media project for homeless children in Washington, D.C. He photographed the "Portraits of the Powerless" show, first displayed at the American Institute of Architects. He is a former UPI White

House photographer whose work on the homeless has been shown nationally and in such competitions as the White House News Photographers Show.

Jack F. Kemp

As secretary of the U.S. Department of Housing and Urban Development (HUD), Jack F. Kemp administers a large block of programs affecting the homeless. He was a presidential candidate in the 1988 Republican primaries. Previously he represented Buffalo, New York, in the U.S. House of Representatives. He was elected to office after a career as a professional football player.

S. Anna Kondratas

S. Anna Kondratas is assistant HUD secretary for community development and planning. She was previously administrator of the Food and Nutrition Service of the U.S. Department of Agriculture and was responsible for the Food Stamp and Women, Infants, and Children (WIC) nutrition program. Kondratas was formerly the Schultz senior policy analyst in health and urban affairs at the Heritage Foundation, where she was a public spokesperson on homelessness and government policy.

Stewart B. McKinney

Representative Stewart B. McKinney, for whom the McKinney Homeless Assistance Act was named, was a Republican member of the House of Representatives at the time of his death from AIDS in 1987. McKinney represented Connecticut's 4th District for more than 16 years. From 1983 until his death, he was the ranking Republican member of the Banking Subcommittee on Housing and Community Development, where he fought to preserve domestic programs in the 1980s.

Samuel Pierce

Samuel Pierce was secretary of the U.S. Department of Housing and Urban Development under President Ronald Reagan. He was the only Cabinet officer to serve both full terms. He was previously a partner in the law firm of Battle, Fowler, Jaffin, Pierce, and Kheel in New York City. He was also general counsel to the U.S. Treasury. Subsequent to his tenure as HUD secretary, it was revealed in a HUD and congressional investigation that numerous HUD programs under his administration suffered significant losses due to poor management and were subject to influence-peddling.

Rebecca Smith

Rebecca Smith, a homeless woman, froze to death in a box on a New York City street corner in 1982. Her death received extensive press coverage after it was discovered that the 61-year-old woman, hospitalized repeatedly for schizophrenia, had been visited by at least 50 people who sought to give her food and shelter during the last weeks of her life. Smith, a mother and once valedictorian of her college class, was declared an "endangered adult" under the city's protective services law; she died before the order could take effect and remove her from the street.

Mitch Snyder

Mitch Snyder is a member of the Community for Creative Non-Violence (CCNV) in Washington, D.C., which he joined in 1973 to open a small shelter for homeless people who would otherwise be held in jail because they lacked a home address. Snyder had previously spent 27 months in federal prison, where he was influenced by many antiwar activists. Snyder has committed numerous acts of nonviolent civil disobedience, has fasted, and has lived on the streets for extended periods of time. He coauthored *Homelessness in America: A Forced March to Nowhere*; he is a well-known activist and speaker on poverty and homelessness.

Chris Sprowal

Chris Sprowal was a founder and first president of the National Union of the Homeless. He was cofounder of the Committee for Dignity and Fairness for the Homeless in Philadelphia, a self-help advocacy and service organization that is managed and operated by homeless and previously homeless people. It was formed in October 1983. Sprowal is a graduate of New York University in engineering. He was an organizer of the 1984 convention of the homeless, whose motto was "Homeless but Not Helpless."

Louisa Stark

Louisa Stark was a founder and president of the National Coalition for the Homeless, serving from 1984–1989. She currently chairs the Consortium for the Homeless in Phoenix, where she is an adjunct professor in the department of anthropology at Arizona State University. She was formerly professor of anthropology at the University of Wisconsin and has served as director of anthropology at the Heard Museum in Phoenix. She served on the Committee on Health Care for Homeless People of the Institute of Medicine, National Academy of Sciences.

John Talbot

John Talbot, M.D., is professor of psychiatry at Cornell University Medical College and associate medical director of the Payne Whitney Psychiatric Clinic at New York Hospital in New York City. He has written widely on the problems of the homeless mentally ill.

E. Fuller Torrey

E. Fuller Torrey is an author as well as a clinical and research psychiatrist in Washington, D.C. His specialty is schizophrenia. For five years in the early 1970s, Torrey was special assistant to the director of the National Institute of Mental Health; subsequently he spent eight years as a staff psychiatrist at Saint Elizabeths Hospital in Washington, D.C. He has extensive professional experience with homeless women.

4

Documents and Reports

THE HOMELESSNESS THAT BEGAN to burst into the awareness of Americans in the early 1980s was of a kind not seen before; it was more complex, generated from more sources and affecting more people. The first general public and governmental acknowledgment of this new problem came as the result of a series of highly publicized congressional hearings, which also served as some of the first national gatherings of the few advocates, researchers, and service providers who were working with the homeless.

Then, as now, the complex problem of homelessness is perhaps best understood in the words of those living closest to it: the homeless themselves, and those who serve them. Thus, this chapter—whose goal is to provide a documentary portrait of some major facets of homelessness—draws initially on the firsthand words of some of those who were seeing and experiencing homelessness up close: in the words of shelter providers; in the words of a homeless and disabled chambermaid who was never offered housing assistance; in the impassioned plea of a researcher who frequented the alleys and subway tunnels of New York City to understand the problem; and in the sober description of a homeless child forced to live in the violent, drug-infested world of a welfare hotel.

In one sense, these firsthand offerings describe the "problem." They are followed by some readings filled with information of a different kind: facts generated by congressional studies, research organizations, and official commissions. These excerpts focus on the realities facing specific groups of the homeless—alcoholics, the mentally ill, school-age children—and on the obstacles presented in meeting such basic human needs as adequate nutrition and permanent housing.

Firsthand Perspectives on Homelessness

Testimony before the Housing Subcommittee

In December 1982, the U.S. Congress convened the first hearing on homelessness since the Great Depression. The first witnesses to testify before the Housing Subcommittee of Representative Henry B. Gonzalez were Mary Ellen Hombs and Mitch Snyder of the Washington, D.C.-based Community for Creative Non-Violence. With their testimony they released *Homelessness in America: A Forced March to Nowhere,* a groundbreaking look at a new and growing problem. With them to the witness table Hombs and Snyder brought the cremated ashes of "John Doe," one of the many homeless people who had frozen to death in the city. This excerpt is from their testimony.

Americans, more than many people, are severely addicted to some very dangerous myths. Yet, we cannot address reality, or hope to change it, until we free ourselves from the fables that entrap us. Perhaps nowhere is this more true than in regard to homeless people. To see them clearly, to understand what their existence says about us personally and collectively, and to comprehend what their needs are requires this: we must face facts as they are, peel away stereotypical prejudices and delusions, boil off foggy thinking, and listen to the voices of those who have known and seen.

We must work from a single point: this is America, 1982. Homelessness is a national problem of massive and increasing proportions, affecting at least two million people.[1] As a fabric, it is made up of the consequences of a number of elements and conditions basic to the way our nation and our society function. We do not always choose to see these clearly, but we will examine them here in as current, authentic, and non-academic a fashion as we can.

It is significant that only two years have elapsed since we prepared the report for Congress. In that time, homelessness has begun to smolder and then ignite as a national issue. The signs of our time can be read in a few events.

Big Red used to be a professional country and western guitarist. Now he is middle-aged and an alcoholic. After eight years of living on Washington's outdoor heat grates, Red's hands are so badly burned that his fingers make crackling sounds when he moves them. His usual place of residence is the grate at the Corcoran Art Gallery. Surrounded by billowing clouds of steam, in a scene reminiscent of Dante's "Inferno," Red needs only to look up to see the home of his nearest neighbor: the President of the United States.

In March 1982, a photo of Red on his grate ran in a two-page story on the homeless in *U.S. News and World Report*. The story was one of several similarly-timed accounts. Among others, "60 Minutes," *Newsweek*, "The McNeil-Lehrer Report," and *The Christian Science Monitor* have carried feature pieces. If the winter of 1981–1982 represented anything, it was an incalculable multiplication of media focus on the homeless. Most stories served the useful purpose of throwing a rope into the quicksand of our illusions, offering us a first step out of our ignorance. If we listened and read carefully, we could know that the traditional and persistent picture of street people as "dirty, lazy, drunken bums" bears scant resemblance to today's chronically homeless person. Wino, tramp, hobo: these are images from another era.

Homeless people are a complex group; their identities and the circumstances of their "previous" lives frequently do not match conventional stereotypes. Thus, shock meets the announcement of the opening of a free soup line for destitute children under age twelve in Washington, D.C. Among the first guests was a three-year-old boy accompanying a seventeen-month-old. Within three weeks, "Martha's Table" was serving thirty children a day in a neighborhood that, not surprisingly and not untypically, has seen little change since it hosted the 1968 riots.

If these events awaken us to reality and to action, we must remember that others have paid with their lives to make it so.

> There may be a message in the 34-year-old Chicago man who was killed recently when the out-of-order trash compactor in which he had been sleeping for weeks was mended without his knowing it and the man, having conceived of himself as an ally of refuse and having been for all practical purposes refuse, finally became refuse and was compacted. But if there is a message, I'm not sure that I want to know what it is. (Ebenezer Hob, "Confessions," *Washingtonian*, July 1978.)

There is indeed a message contained in the life and death of the man from Chicago, just as there is in the story of Big Red and Martha's Table. And, as Ebenezer Hob confesses, most people are not quite certain that they want to know what it is. The discussion, documentation, and reflections on homelessness offered here are for those who realize that they must decipher that message, regardless of where it may lead.

Note

1. No one can say with certainty how many people in this nation are homeless. Not until they come inside will we know for certain how many there are. However,

in 1980, we prepared a report, for a Congressional committee, on the national dimensions of the problem. At that time, we concluded that approximately 1 percent of the population, or 2.2. million people, lacked shelter. We arrived at that conclusion on the basis of information received from more than 100 agencies and organizations in 25 cities and states. That figure has since been widely used by the media, politicos, and organizers. It is as accurate an estimate as anyone in the country could offer, yet it lacks absolute statistical certainty.

In gathering information for this book, we have learned nothing that would cause us to lower our original estimate. In fact, we would increase it, since we are convinced that the number of homeless people in the United States could reach 3 million or more during 1983.

Source: From *Homelessness in America: A Forced March to Nowhere,* by Mary Ellen Hombs and Mitch Snyder. Published by the Community for Creative Non-Violence, Washington, DC, 1983. pp. xvi–xviii.

Testimony of May Ash

On January 25, 1984, members of the Subcommittee on Housing and Community Development of the Committee on Banking, Finance and Urban Affairs, U.S. House of Representatives, held a one-day hearing, "Homelessness in America-II" as a follow up to the hearing of December 1982, which was the first on homelessness since the Great Depression. The follow-up hearing was held in the basement of the CCNV-operated shelter in Washington, D.C. This excerpt is from the transcript of the hearings, pp. 19–20.

Among those testifying was May Ash, a woman in her late fifties who had worked as a chambermaid at the Waldorf Astoria hotel in New York City and as a maid for many years. She lost her job and spent six years living in Grand Central Station. At the time of the hearing, she was staying at a church shelter across the street from the Waldorf. May Ash's statement was interrupted several times by her tears. Crying, with a stocking hat pulled over her hair, hers was the face captured by the press and flashed around the nation as the hearing was reported.

My name is May Elizabeth Ash, I am from New York City. I am fifty-six years old. I have been homeless for two years. And I have been living in shelters here and there. Most of my friends that is in the shelters have died and I have seen them come, and been sick at the hospital.

At the age that I am, and with one eye plus other ailments, I am a diabetic, they wouldn't have hired me for work. I wouldn't mind having a job if they would give it to me. Being homeless is not a thing that I would like. I would rather be somewhere else than to be in a shelter for the rest of my life. . . .

I used to live in Philadelphia before I came to New York. And it was just as rough there as it is here in New York. . . .

In the street there, sleeping in bus stations, train stations, doorways, different places. I go to welfare and they wouldn't help me. They tell me I ain't old enough. . . .

I don't have enough money to pay for the places they would like for me to have. The rent is so high.

Mr. Schumer. The rent was too high for the amount of money that you had?

Ms. Ash. Yes, it was.

Mr. Schumer. Did anyone ever come to you and say you could get some kind of assistance, either public housing or Section 8? No one has ever suggested to you or come to you and said they would help you fill out the forms and all of that?

Ms. Ash. Not ever.

Mr. Schumer. Do you receive public assistance? Do you receive welfare?

Ms. Ash. I don't receive welfare. I just started receiving social security disability.

Mr. Schumer. You just started getting that?

Ms. Ash. Yes.

Mr. Schumer. Was there a person that you had to see to fill out all the forms and get the check?

Ms. Ash. Yes.

Mr. Schumer. They never suggested to you, they never tried to give you any help in finding housing?

Ms. Ash. No.

Mr. Schumer. So you really are sort of bereft?

Ms. Ash. Yes, I am.

Testimony of Kim Hopper

Kim Hopper, one of the two New York City researchers who provided the first profiles of the homeless of the 1980s in that city, like May Ash testified at the 1984 Homelessness in America-II hearing. With his research colleague, Ellen Baxter, and Robert Hayes, the counsel of the National Coalition for the Homeless, Hopper had testified at the first congressional hearing. This excerpt is from the transcript of the hearing, pp. 192–194.

... As you will hear repeatedly today, the plight of our homeless has gone from bad to worse since December 1982. Part of this Nation is now enjoying a modest economic recovery; at the same time legions of this country's men, women, and children suffer the misery of hunger, of homelessness, of acute want among plenty.

Are we helping? A little bit. There are, today, more soup kitchens and more emergency shelters from coast to coast, than at any time since the Great Depression. But even these valiant relief efforts—staffed in large part by volunteers—have not arrested the growth of the vast army of the very poor in America's streets. The mills of homelessness grind on, unabated by our puny efforts at makeshift remedies. Despite tentative signs of an economic upturn, ... the plain fact is that there are many more Americans homeless today than there were a year ago.

Homelessness in America ... is no longer a shameful secret. So why isn't something being done? No one doubts that we have the expertise to house the homeless. No one doubts that this Nation's wealth is sufficient to accord the poor, at the very least, the resources needed for survival. The clamor on the streets is a desperate plea for help. So why must the homeless poor continue to plead their case for elementary justice, for decency? Why have we refused to mobilize the minimal reserves needed to alleviate this crisis? ... [I]n those questions lies an indictment of the state of the moral values of our Nation, of our government, of ourselves.

Last summer Tiffany's, the Fifth Avenue jeweler, put up a window display advertising a fifty thousand dollar necklace. The backdrop: Figurines depicting homeless people, surrounded by trash. Tiffany's management seemed to think trivializing human misery might amuse its clientele. Last fall, the Holiday Inn threw a party for its executives in Chicago. The corporation hired an actress to ramble around the reception posed as a "bag lady." Amusing? I am sure most of you recall the Fort Lauderdale official who proposed spraying garbage with poison to prevent the poor from scrounging for scraps.

And, perhaps most disturbing of all, over the past year certain parties have come to argue that growing numbers of the homeless are not "truly homeless"; they suggest some homeless folks simply do not deserve assistance. Alarmingly, such a position cannot be dismissed as the ravings of a few cranks or eccentrics. Ideologically extreme they may be, but their arguments find an audience. New York City's mayor, for one, is a self-proclaimed disciple of this doctrine.

It is this brand of callousness, which has permitted our Government—the Congress, the President, States and cities, too—to preside over the spectacle of two million Americans homeless and to do next to nothing. What do we think, what do we hope our children and grandchildren will say of our complicity in watching the slow suffering—and, in due time, death—of the weakest and frailest of our fellow citizens. What can we do? What must we do? To begin with, I continue to believe that the only way the homeless will find relief is through (1) their own actions, and (2) the good will and fundamental decency of the American people. I do not expect any longer to find that decency within the higher leadership of this Government. I do believe that once America looks at the face of the homeless, into the eyes of a homeless person, it will not turn away. Once educated as to the reality of homelessness, the vast majority of people of good will will recognize that homelessness is unacceptable, and will demand that it be ended. It will accept the homelessness for what it is and demand that it end. Then, and I fear only then, will Government act.

This committee, I submit, could help ignite this spirit of decency in America. A year ago we came to Capitol Hill to tell you of homelessness. Homeless people, too, came to your Chambers to share with you their lives. You are to be commended for coming off the Hill and coming to an emergency shelter for today's hearing. You bring the Congress close to the problem. More of this needs to be done.

I conclude with a few modest proposals. . . . Isn't it about time for Congress to consider a national right to shelter? Let it be debated. Let the administration tell Congress how much it will cost. And then let us tell you how much homelessness costs, in dollars, in human lives and in a degraded sense of our own humanity. In 1977 Parliament enacted a Homeless Persons Act in the United Kingdom, guaranteeing a right to shelter for at least some of the British homeless. Seven years later can we not do as much? I invite the committee to work with us to draft the legislation. I ask this committee . . . to introduce it. I would welcome the opportunity to press the opponents of the legislation on what they would offer the homeless instead.

I am sometimes shamed by how little we ask for: Is it too much to expect a right to shelter at least for homeless children, probably the fastest growing group among the homeless? Can we not, immediately, shelter them? It would not, I submit, be so difficult to amend the Social Security Act to make mandatory the provision of emergency shelter under the assistance to families with dependent children program.

Second, how long will the Congress ignore the plight of the homeless mentally ill. Again, the answer is not to reopen the asylum gates and force these frail people into lives of relentless incarceration. We know how to care for the mentally ill in the community. . . .

It is not so expensive, once a residence is established, for there are ongoing income support programs—such as, with all its current problems, the SSI program. Even if public housing is going the way of the dinosaur under this administration, can we not prevail upon the Government to support housing for the most helpless and neediest of the poor and homeless? I would urge the committee to push for a special capital program to create permanent supportive housing for the homeless mentally disabled.

Lastly, one cannot speak to this housing committee without reiterating the obvious. The root cause of homelessness absent which all the competing causes could be accommodated is the scarcity of low-income housing. Unless the Federal Government helps there, all our efforts to alleviate homelessness are bound to failure. This committee is to be commended for its efforts to salvage at least some housing programs from the wrecker's ball. But you know better than I how inadequate those efforts have been. You have heard something today about the effects of homelessness on those who endure it. What does it say about our moral integrity, about our values, about our priorities if we continue—as individuals and as a society—to walk past the old woman living on the corner, sleeping in a cardboard box?

There is a vicious Darwinian struggle going on in this country, a desperate competition for housing. As in any free market competition, it is the weak who are losing—the infirm, the elderly, the ill educated, the unemployed, the single parent families.

Each day we permit the weak to lose their struggle for survival resources, we are cheapened. Each day we permit homelessness to continue, we display our own moral shabbiness. Each day a fellow American succumbs to the cold on a city street, our national legitimacy as a civilized society is thrown into question.

Testimony of Yvette Diaz

Women and children represent one of the fastest-growing segments of the homeless population. Inadequate housing resources and governmental funding requirements have often resulted in these families being sheltered in "welfare hotels," rented spaces in run-down buildings in dangerous areas. A special congressional hearing on the plight of homeless children heard this testimony from a child living in the notorious Hotel Martinique in New York City.

My name is Yvette Diaz. I am twelve years old. I live in the Martinique Hotel, Forty-nine West Thirty-second Street, New York City. I live in rooms 1107 to 1108. There are two rooms. I live here with my mother, two sisters, nine and seven, and my three year old brother. We have lived in the Martinique Hotel for almost two years now. I am living at the Martinique Hotel because my aunt's house burned down, and we didn't have any place to live.

We were living in my aunt's house in Brooklyn because my father was discharged from the United States Air Force in the State of Washington, and the family came back to New York where we originally came from. We couldn't find an apartment right away, so we stayed with my aunt. Then, the house burned down, and we went to the Martinique Hotel.

Since we are living in New York at the Martinique, I have been going to P.S. 64, which is on East Sixth Street in Manhattan. When I first started school here, I was absent a lot, because the bus that took us to

school in the mornings was late a lot of times, and other times I didn't
get up on time. We didn't have an alarm clock. Finally, my mother saved
up enough to buy one. This year I have not been absent many times
because the bus is on time, and we have an alarm clock.

I don't like the hotel, because there is always a lot of trouble there.
Many things happen that make me afraid. I don't go down into the street
to play, because there is no place to play on the streets. The streets are
dangerous, with all kinds of sick people who are on drugs or crazy. My
mother is afraid to let me go downstairs. Only this Saturday, my friend,
the security guard at the hotel, Mr. Santiago, was killed on my floor. He
was shot by another man and killed. The blood is still on the walls and
on the floor. Anyway, people are afraid to open the door to even look
out. There are a lot of people on drugs in the hotel. Sometimes you can
find needles and other things that drugs come in, all over the hallways.

Our apartment was broken into when we were out. They stole the
radio and our telephone alarm clock [sic]. We have a TV but they didn't
get that, because we hide it in the closet under other things every time we
leave the room.

We can't cook in the apartment. My mother sneaked a hot plate in,
because we don't have enough money to eat out every night. They, the
hotel, warned us that if we are caught cooking in the rooms, we could be
sent to a shelter. I play in the hallways with my friends from other rooms
on my floor. Sometimes, even that isn't safe. A boy, about fifteen or
sixteen, came over to me and wanted to take me up to the sixteenth floor.
I got frightened and ran into my room and told my mother. She went to
the police and she was told this same boy was showing his private parts
to girls before, and that it was reported to them. If he bothered me again,
I was to tell the police.

The five of us live in two rooms at this hotel. There is only one
bathroom. We don't have mice or rats like some of the other people who
live in the hotel, because we have a cat.

I go to the extended day program at my school, P.S. 64. We go from
3:00 to 6:00 every weekday except Friday. I get help with my homework
for 45 minutes every day and then we have computer, arts and crafts,
dancing, gym, and game room. I like it and we also get a hot dinner
every night before we go home on the bus. I finish all my homework here
as the teacher helps me and it is quiet so I can really understand what I
am doing.

If I could have anything that I want, I wish that we had our own
apartment in a nice, clean building and a place that I could go outside to
play in that is safe. I want that most of all for me and my family.

Thank you.

Source: From *The Crisis in Homelessness: Effects on Children and Families.*
Select Committee on Children, Youth, and Families, U.S. House of Representatives, 100th Cong., 1st sess., 1987. pp. 9–10.

Hunger and the Homeless

Many facts of homeless life debilitate the person trying to survive without shelter: inadequate clothing, no opportunity to rest, no access to health care, the endless travel to seek services, the search for food. Some people are forced to scavenge for scraps, others regularly visit soup kitchens. The following reading describes some congressional findings about the homeless and their search for food.

Major Findings from Shelter Provider Survey

I. Primary Sources of Food for the Homeless

Eight-one percent (81%) of shelter providers state that the private sector meals at shelters are a primary source of food for homeless persons; yet most (52%) shelters do not provide two main meals daily. . . . For the purpose of this report "two main meals" are defined as lunch and dinner which generally provide at least one-half an individual's daily nutrient requirements. Typically, the homeless must seek out food in soup kitchens when they are accessible, from dumpsters, and other free food sites. Dumpsters are cited as a primary source of food for the homeless by nine percent (9%) of shelter providers.

II. Large Percentage of Homeless Not Receiving Food Stamps

Forty-five percent (45%) of the total number of homeless persons identified as eligible for food stamps (1,678 out of 3,751) were reported not to be receiving benefits. Among the homeless in family shelters, forty-nine percent (49%) of those identified as eligible (1,028 out of 2,112) were reported not to be receiving food stamps. In shelters with no one available to assist in the food stamp application process, fifty-eight percent (58%) of the homeless identified as eligible were reported not to be receiving food stamps (225 out of 440).

III. Administrative Barriers to Food Stamp Participation

Twenty-one percent (21%) of shelter providers reported their homeless residents are denied eligibility for food stamps because they do not have a permanent address or are sleeping outside.

Sixty-seven percent (67%) of responding shelter providers (60 out of 90) reported their homeless residents experience lengthy delays in between applying for food stamps and receipt of benefits.

Documentation problems were the greatest single reported barrier to participation in the Food Stamp Program for eligible homeless. Twenty-five percent (25%) of shelters reporting lengthy delays (13 out of 53) cited inadequate documentation as the cause. For fourteen percent (14%) of all shelters, inadequate documentation was not only a barrier or a cause of lengthy delay, but was reported to result in denial of food stamps for eligible homeless persons.

The need for increased assistance to the homeless in applying for food stamps and the use of more shelter providers as collateral contacts in the application process is supported by the survey findings of administrative barriers to food stamp participation.

IV. Shelter Providers Approve Use of Food Stamps by Homeless for Prepared Meals at Soup Kitchens and/or Shelters

Sixty-five percent (65%) of all responding shelter providers would like to see the utility of food stamps for the homeless improved by allowing them to purchase or contribute to the cost of prepared meals at shelters and/or soup kitchens with food stamps—as recently authorized in Public Law 99-570, the Omnibus Drug Enforcement, Education and Control Act (enacted October 27, 1986). The providers support this change in law primarily because they believe it would greatly improve the quality and quantity of food assistance available to the homeless.

Moreover, many providers state that this change in statute can remove another "barrier" to food stamp participation in some areas. By allowing shelters to be certified as institutions eligible to accept food stamps, the food stamp rule denying eligibility to institutional residents will be lifted for homeless persons in certified shelters.

V. Hunger Related Health Problems Reported Among Shelter Residents

Hunger related health problems reported among the homeless include: anemia, infectious diseases, low birthweight, chronic diseases requiring special diets (hypertension and diabetes), lack of infant formula, and children appearing physically underdeveloped for their age. (These reports of health problems by nonmedical shelter providers parallel the findings of many published medical reports on the health problems of the homeless.)

Source: From *Hunger Among the Homeless: A Survey of 140 Shelters, Food Stamp Participation and Recommendations.* Select Committee on Hunger, U.S. House of Representatives, 100th Cong., 1st sess., 1987. pp. 4–5.

Alcoholism and the Homeless

Alcoholism is the traditional characteristic associated with the homeless of yesteryear, but it does not involve more than 30 percent of the current homeless population, which is more diverse. Treat-

ment for alcoholism, as for drug problems, is difficult to obtain for
the poor person, even more difficult for the person with no home at
all. This reading describes some of the alcohol recovery programs
available for the homeless.

Common Themes and Issues among Service Programs

Generally speaking, providers of comprehensive programs consider their
services to consist of three major components. These components cover
the intake, primary recovery, and sustained recovery aspects of the
process of recovering from alcohol problems mainly through achieving
and maintaining sobriety. Recovery program operators are the first to
admit that theirs is an imperfect system that too often fails to attract or
hold clients to the point that the individual is able to establish long-term
sobriety and continuing recovery. Hope, continued effort to make
services available, and encouragement of the client's motivation and
desire to help one's self, are mainstays of the programs' operations.

1. *Intake services.* Special efforts are taken to make services available to
homeless people with alcohol problems who are seen to need them, but
resist accepting them. Special emphasis is placed on outreach and intake
services. Three types of outreach were observed—active outreach (e.g.,
seeking out clients by positioning staff in shelters, or through mobile
patrols), passive outreach (e.g., day-time drop-in centers located in skid
row), and protective custody (e.g., transport (possibly involuntary) of
public inebriates to sobering stations or detoxification centers).

　Intake services occur through shelters, sobering stations,
detoxification facilities, hospitals, jails, and residential recovery settings.
Traditional "revolving door" problems of public inebriates who
repeatedly utilize police, hospital, missions, emergency rooms, and
alcohol recovery programs are still present, although markedly reduced
from past levels by the funneling of such utilization through sobering
stations and detoxification facilities.

2. *Primary recovery programs.* Recovery programs' emphasis is chiefly
upon establishing sobriety and working for the individual's personal
recovery from alcohol problems. Following intake/detoxification,
primary recovery occurs through didactic, social, and spiritual
approaches carried out in a residential setting where the client is
encouraged to make a personal commitment to sobriety and to a lifetime
of recovery through an alcohol-free lifestyle. Alcoholics Anonymous is
almost always a critical element in these programs.

　Programs for chronic public inebriates tend to be longer in duration
(three to six months or longer), to put more emphasis upon restoration
of physical and mental functioning, and to provide more vocational and
domestic supports, than is customary for residential recovery programs

serving the general population of people with alcohol problems. The goals for the individual remain fixed on achieving sobriety and self-sufficiency to the fullest extent possible. Relapses almost always require re-entry into the program from the beginning.

The basic recovery process is generally considered the same for homeless people with drinking problems as for all other problem drinkers. Although some programs put more emphasis on homelessness than others (and these were the ones sought out for this study), nearly all publicly-funded alcohol programs serve clients who experience homelessness, or incipient homelessness. Homelessness comes in all shades and varieties in association with alcohol problems, from the person habituated to living on the streets to the recently-fired executive just evicted by a spouse. Accordingly, and wisely, alcohol service program providers are generally less concerned with the type or degree of homelessness than they are with the client's willingness to enter the recovery process.

3. *Sustained recovery.* Support and follow-up services are necessary to assure that the individual's full range of needs is met, and that all is done that can be to help the individual maintain sobriety. Support services include health, mental health, vocational, educational, legal, veterans', and housing and welfare services.

Programs vary in degree of emphasis on this, but all expect the client to be active in seeking out these services for him or herself. If the client is too debilitated to do so, efforts will probably be made to transfer the client to that service (e.g., to transfer a psychotic client to a mental health program). Unfortunately, if the transfer cannot be made, the client may be discharged in any case to "independent living." Achieving such transfers for a homeless person without insurance, especially for someone who's [*sic*] drinking has not been stopped or stabilized, is often extremely difficult.

Within this general progression of care, several themes and issues emerged from the study:

1. Public policy is lacking for service to homeless people with alcohol problems. Coherent local policies are usually lacking, and national policies have not been formally articulated by any national-level organizations, for prevention and treatment of alcohol problems among the homeless. With the exception of recommendations from two NIAAA-sponsored conferences in 1985 and 1987, formal statements on the subject have not been issued. People with alcohol problems are often subsumed in general statements of concern about the homeless, but are not thereby assured of alcohol-problem recovery services. The absence of national leadership on alcohol and homelessness requires entrepreneurship and initiative by local alcohol programs to establish their own visibility and entree into local planning activity for the homeless (see Point 8 below).

2. Homeless people with alcohol problems in the 1980s are a far more diverse group than the traditional "older white male skid row alcoholic." More younger people, more minorities, and more women, more poly-drug use, and more mental illness, and people with less education and fewer vocational skills, now comprise the population of homeless people with alcohol problems. Alcohol service programs report increasing contacts with these new groups. Some programs are feeling their way on their own initiatives to establish new programs for them (e.g., special programs for homeless women). Developing new services for the homeless has been slow in the absence of service utilization studies, lack of epidemiological and demographic data, and without any special mandates or funding from public or private sources of support.

3. Formal, critical evaluation of program activities is rarely done, and is not generally required by funding agencies. Most alcohol service programs keep records on service utilization by clients. However, the records seem to be used more for certifying contract performance to funding sources than for critical study to further development of services. No formal mechanisms exist to encourage service providers to trade notes and learn from one another's experiences, although programs do know about each other. How much contact they have and how much they learn from each other is difficult to determine.

4. Programs generally develop on their own initiative based on local conditions and upon the orientations and backgrounds of the program's leadership. Program directors often have been associated with their program for ten years or more. Several directors were also founders of the program, or have been with the program from the beginning. Individuals' strengths and abilities are major sources for program innovations and competence. This leadership can lead to new programs which often spin off from older, well-established programs. . . .

5. Controversy exists over the proper use of protective services for public drinkers who might be a danger to self or others. Decriminalization of public drunkenness and the advent of "non-medical" or "social-model" detoxification services have raised questions about when the police and health authorities may intervene to remove a person involuntary [sic] in episodes of public drinking and public drunkenness. Police are generally cordial to relaxed handling of public inebriates [sic], working under arrangements in which police are far more likely to transport inebriates to the alcohol program (notably the sobering station/detoxification center) than to jail. The cordiality can mask civil liberties issues that flare up when an inebriate does not want to be moved. The issues may come more to the fore if more local jurisdictions deputize alcohol-program workers . . . to take public inebriates into custody for transportation to an alcohol program.

6. Coordination of mental health and alcohol services for homeless people is often lacking. People with alcohol problems who also have

mental health problems are not likely to be served, even though the psychiatric problems may be readily treatable, if trained mental health staff are not available. The recent advent of specialized "dual diagnosis" programs is a response to gaps in care between mental health and alcohol recovery programs. The problems are philosophical as well as technical. Some deep differences exist between the two fields regarding use of drugs during treatment and regarding staff training and qualifications. Some alcohol programs emphasize completely drug-free environments in contrast to mental health programs that rely on medication to stabilize their clients. Some alcohol programs with a strong self-help orientation are reluctant to accept mental health services with strong clinical and professional orientations, and vice versa.

7. Integrated city-wide planning and delivery of alcohol recovery services in conjunction with shelters and other public programs is rare. . . . More often, it appears that individual alcohol programs develop a network of ad-hoc referral relationships with other helping agencies on an as-needed basis. This informal approach may achieve many of the benefits of integrated planning without some of the costs involved in large-scale coordination. But the informal approach also may be wasteful and may fail to make important connections between services. To our knowledge, little study has been devoted to the development of linkages between alcohol programs to coordinate and integrate service delivery.

8. Initiative by the alcohol program agency is required to secure linkages to adjunct services. With one exception, non-alcohol agencies do not accept responsibility to assure linkage between alcohol recovery services and other human services that are important for recovery. These services include health care; mental health care; vocational/education assistance; qualifications for benefits and entitlements; advocacy; legal services; protection and security; physically disabled; multiple problems. The exception is the Pew/Johnson "Health Care for the Homeless" program. In several cities, HCH medical teams have been vigorous in providing mobile outreach and clinic services in conjunction with alcohol-problem recovery services. Further study is recommended of models and strategies for effective use of other human services during the recovery process.

9. Staffing and manpower issues revolve around the integration of "clinical" approaches relying on trained people from the helping professions and "experiential" approaches to service that rely on self-help. . . . Program environments that expected the client to act vigorously on his or her own behalf usually provide both kinds of support.

10. Program organization and leadership. Creation of an environment conducive to recovery is a major theme of program organization. Recovery environments simultaneously emphasize the dignity and importance of the individual, and provide a milieu in which sobriety and principles of community living serve to establish norms for the program participants.

The program's director is usually as concerned about the quality of the environment as he or she is about the quality of treatment services and counseling at the individual level.

11. Program leadership comes from diverse backgrounds. Program leaders' backgrounds are diverse professionally and in terms of life history, including both recovering individuals and professionally trained individuals from many different disciplinary backgrounds. Personal qualities are important, and flexibility and approachability are important characteristics.

12. Sound community relations are critical to successful program operations. Alcohol programs serving the homeless must answer to their neighbors as well as to their funding sources (who often are community organizations to begin with). Strategies for maintaining solid relationships include: creation of strong local boards; cultivation of local political and institutional leadership; careful attention to review procedures and community involvement in securing sites for program facilities; and positive, active participation in community events.

13. Alcohol programs serving the homeless recognize the need to eliminate conditions that create homelessness. Most of the programs studied recognize the importance of socio-economic factors in homelessness, and several are working to deal with local conditions while they are providing services to individuals. Denial of access to housing for low-income people and to jobs that pay a liveable wage are recognized as structural problems that inhibit recovery. Some programs . . . have taken initiative to increase access to housing and jobs as part of their program activities.

14. Alcohol programs are working to provide safety and support services for homeless people who continue to drink. Alcohol programs participate in the struggle of all who work to eradicate homelessness and who try to make communities safer and more tolerable for homeless people. Alcohol programs with strong community-service mandates . . . are working to increase housing, protection and street-oriented services.

A number of program directors and other observers believe that creation of places to accommodate the "homeless inebriate" in the community would relieve pressure on the existing alcohol service system. Such accommodation would decrease demand on basic shelter and protection services that could be provided more expeditiously in other settings. For example, supervised wet hotels and sobering stations, day-use occupancy of night shelters, and other walk-in day-use facilities might relieve the use of detoxification and emergency services. More facilities that can accept mail, provide spot jobs, telephones, clothes, lockers, showers and laundry, would make it easier for people to look after themselves. Community outreach work with liquor-store operators, bartenders, hotel owners, store-owners, police, case-managers, and others who come in contact with public inebriates can help protect inebriates and link them up with services.

Source: From National Institute on Alcohol Abuse and Alcoholism (NIAAA). *Alcohol Recovery Programs for Homeless People: A Survey of Current Programs in the U.S.,* 1988. pp. 2–6.

Mental Illness and the Homeless

The homeless mentally ill are some of the most visible and easily identified of those on the streets. Most studies have found that about 30 percent of the homeless have some mental illness. This reading describes some of the necessary services for this population.

First, in our country the number of seriously and chronically mentally ill among the homeless is staggering (from 20 to 80 percent of the estimated 750,000 to 3 million homeless, depending on where the study was done, live in the streets or in shelters). . . . [U]ntil recently the homeless were largely regarded as shiftless, poor, alcohol-abusing vagabonds. In recent years, however, their numbers have included an increasing number and percentage of persons suffering from serious and chronic (long-term) mental illnesses: primarily schizophrenia, unresponsive psychotic depression and organic mental illness. Even taking a conservative figure of 20 percent, we are talking about a great number, and the number and percent who have been in state mental hospitals is even higher.

When you look at the homeless mentally ill, realize that you are dealing with two problems with multiple causes and subgroups: *homelessness and chronic mental illnesses.* Each, in and of itself, is a formidable challenge to resolve, but combined, they present a problem of unprecedented magnitude and complexity. The population bears the cross of a dual disenfranchisement from society and its agents of service delivery: the mentally ill are often excluded from programs designed to serve the homeless, and those who are homeless are typically screened out from receiving services designed for the chronically mentally ill. The homeless mentally ill have become our society's "untouchables," unable to advocate for themselves, unable to protect themselves from harm, unable to acquire the bare necessities of living.

Recently, as reported on the front page of the May 22, 1989, *New York Times,* alcohol and drug addiction have emerged as another major reason for the homelessness of men, women, and families. Many of the chronically mentally ill are also addicted to either drugs or alcohol. The crack cocaine epidemic has certainly increased the numbers of the homeless above our earlier estimates at the time of the APA's Task Force Report. As reported in the *Times*, experts who are finding a substantial drug problem among the homeless found that close to 50 percent of the homeless men living in downtown Los Angeles were addicts and 75 percent of men arriving at the Franklin Street shelter in the South Bronx were addicts. However, tragically, treatment programs are virtually non-existent. While there are between 50,000 and 100,000 homeless people in Los Angeles County, there are only 20 to 25 beds available for them in residential treatment programs.

Second, for this population, a simple, single housing facility is insufficient. Instead, these disabled citizens require a range of graded, step-wise housing opportunities from large halfway houses to smaller group homes, to individual apartments or homes. As opposed to those out of work, burned out of their homes, etc., the severely and chronically mentally ill cannot resume their full personal, familial, social, vocational and community lives following treatment of their acute phase of illness. They must also slowly recuperate from their illnesses—often progressing from acute inpatient units to chronic state hospitals to rehabilitation programs to day hospitals or half-way houses to group or foster home to independent living—in a slow but progressive manner. Thus, they need a range of housing opportunities, that includes more "restrictive" and larger sized facilities, smaller groups and family homes, and eventually, individual homes or apartments.

. . . [I]n 1955 there were 559,000 patients in state hospitals; today, at any given time, there are approximately 123,000. Conceptually, deinstitutionalization was not flawed; its implementation was. The importance of psychoactive medication and a stable source of financial support was perceived, but the importance of developing such fundamental resources as supportive living arrangements was not clearly seen nor implemented. Nor was it foreseen how reluctant many states would be to allocate funds for community-based services. Almost immediately after deinstitutionalization occurred, society reacted vehemently to the presence of the homeless on our cities' streets. An adequate number and ample range of graded, stepwise, supervised community housing settings must be established. While many of the homeless may benefit from temporary housing such as shelters, and while some portion of the severely chronically mentally ill are able to graduate to independent living, for the vast majority, neither shelters nor mainstream low-cost housing (such as Section 8 or Section 202 housing) are in and of themselves appropriate. Instead, there must be settings offering different levels of supervision, both more and less intensive, including quarterway and halfway houses, lodges and camps, board and care homes, satellite housing, family or foster care, and crisis housing or temporary hotels. Organized and supervised living arrangements can help stabilize the lives of such individuals to a marked extent. Supervision would help ensure that medications are taken, that an address is available for the delivery of SSI, SSDI, Medicare and Medicaid payments, and that there is an address available for case workers and health and supportive care workers.

Third, while affordable, accessible housing is necessary for this population, it is insufficient, absent supervision (ranging from full-time, on-site staff in intensive settings to potentially-frequent visits from visiting nurses, social workers, case managers and the like) when disabled persons are living more independently. They require different levels of supervision and services depending on their degree of residual mental impairment and progressive ability to resume activities of everyday living (shopping, cooking, banking, job-hunting, etc.) They thus require more intensive medical-psychiatric care as they are in the early phase of recuperation, greater full-time staff involvement as they re-enter the community, then continuing follow-up by visiting nurses, social workers and case managers (depending on their individual needs), until they are fully re-established in the "mainstream."

To summarize, *adequate, comprehensive, and accessible psychiatric and rehabilitative services must be available and must be assertively provided through outreach services when needed.*

First, there must be an adequate number of *direct psychiatric services,* both in the streets and in the housing provided, when appropriate, that provide (a) outreach contact with the mentally ill in the community, (b) psychiatric assessment and evaluation, (c) crisis intervention, (d) individualized treatment plans, (e) psychotropic medication and other somatic therapies, and (f) psychosocial treatment. A clear model for this sort of service system was established in the 1980 Mental Health Systems Act. (PL 98-398) though, regrettably, that law was later repealed during the first months of the Reagan Administration.

There must be an adequate number of rehabilitative services providing socialization experiences, training in the skills of everyday living, and social rehabilitation. Programs providing such services could be patterned after day treatment programs, or some of the more social support-related services provided by senior centers. These treatment and rehabilitative services must by provided assertively, for instance, by going out to patients' living settings if they do not or cannot come to a centralized program.

General medical assessment and care must be available. Since we know that the chronically mentally ill have three times the morbidity and mortality of their counterparts of the same age in the general population, and the homeless even higher rates, the ready availability of general medical care is essential and critical. Again, this could occur within the housing sites or within the rehabilitation programs.

Crisis services must be available and accessible to both the chronically mentally ill homeless and the chronically mentally ill in general. Too often, the homeless mentally ill who are in crisis are ignored because they are presumed to reject all conventional forms of help. Even more inappropriately, they may be put into inpatient hospital units when rapid, specific interventions such as medication or crisis housing would be more effective and less costly. Others may be incarcerated in corrections facilities, even more inappropriate and more costly than other settings. Others in need of acute hospitalization are denied it because of restrictive admission criteria or commitment laws. In any case, it will be difficult to provide adequate crisis services to the homeless mentally ill until they are conceptualized and treated separately from the large numbers of other homeless persons.

A system of responsibility for the chronically mentally ill living in the community must be established, with the goal of ensuring that ultimately each patient has one person responsible for his or her care. The shift of psychiatric care from the institutional to community setting does not in any way eliminate the need to continue the provision of comprehensive services to the mentally ill. Indeed, the need for asylum for such persons may be even greater when confronted by the larger community setting. As a result, society must declare a policy of responsibility for the mentally ill who are unable to meet their own needs; governments must designate programs in each region or locality as core agencies responsible and accountable for the care of the chronically mentally ill living there; and the staff of these agencies must be assigned individual patients for whom they are responsible. The ultimate goal must be to ensure that each chronically mentally ill person in this country has one person—a case manager, if you will, who is responsible for his or her treatment and care. The entire burden must not be allowed to fall upon families as if this illness—as compared to physical illness—were their fault and they should be punished.

Source: Edited from Statement of The American Psychiatric Association on S565 "The National Affordable Housing Act," presented by John A. Talbot M.D., Professor and Chairman, Department of Psychiatry, University of Maryland School of Medicine before the Senate Banking and Urban Affairs Committee Subcommittee on Housing and Urban Affairs, June 1, 1989.

Education and Homeless Children

The state of homelessness is a disruptive one and very hard on children, who represent one of the fastest-growing groups of those without shelter. Without a stable permanent home, very little in the way of education is possible. Federal legislation, however, mandates certain actions by the states to guarantee access to education for homeless children. The following reading describes this law.

The Stewart B. McKinney Act

The Stewart B. McKinney Homeless Assistance Act, signed into law on July 22, 1987, provides comprehensive federal emergency assistance for homeless persons. It specifically addresses the barriers to education of homeless children. The Act establishes for the first time a national, uniform policy for the education of homeless children. In addition, the McKinney Act had made available funds for the development of programs to facilitate enrollment and attendance of homeless children in school. These funds, though limited, should help to provide urgently needed relief.

The Act states that, as a matter of federal policy, homeless children are entitled to a free, appropriate public school education. It states that residency requirements may not be used to deny access to such education to homeless children. It specifically directs states to review their residency laws to ensure that those laws do not create barriers to homeless children.

The Act also creates a specific program to fund the implementation of these requirements. Under this program, states establish a "Coordinator of Education of Homeless Children and Youth" and write plans specifying how the educational needs of homeless children will be addressed. The Act requires the plans to address specific barriers faced by homeless children as follows:

1. Residency requirements

The Act states that children will be educated in one of two districts. The Act states that the local education agency of each homeless child or youth shall either a) continue the child's or youth's education in the school district of origin for the remainder of the school year; or b) enroll the child or youth in the school district where the child or youth is actually living; whichever is in the child's best interest or the youth's best interest.[1]

By law the student must be placed in either one school district or the other. In the event that school districts should disagree on the child's "best interest," the state will "provide procedures for the resolution of disputes regarding the educational placement. . . ."[2]

2. Records

The Act calls for efficient handling of records:

> The school records of each homeless child or youth shall be maintained: (A) so that records are available, in a timely manner, when a child or youth enters a new school district. . . .[3]

3. Special Education

Under the Act, homeless children are entitled to special education programs:

Each homeless child shall be provided services comparable to services offered to other students in the school, . . . including educational services for which the child meets the eligibility criteria, such as compensatory educational programs for the disadvantaged, and educational programs for the handicapped and for students with limited English proficiency. . . .[4]

4. Guardianship

The Act facilitates placement of homeless children and youth who do not reside with their parents when it stipulates:

The choice regarding [educational] placement shall be made regardless of whether the child or youth is living with the homeless parents or has been temporarily placed elsewhere by the parents.[5]

In addition to creating a uniform policy to guarantee access to education for homeless children, the McKinney Act also provides funds for states to develop exemplary programs to serve the special needs of homeless children. States may use such funds to formalize coordination, outreach and awareness in their service agencies. All states are encouraged to apply for these funds.[6]

Notes

1. Act, Sec. 722 (e) (3).

2. Id. at Sec. 722 (e) (4).

3. Id. at Sec. 722 (e) (6).

4. Id. at Sec. 722 (e) (5).

5. Id. at Sec. 722 (e) (4).

6. Even small grants can be put to good use. For example, the state of Washington is planning to use its grant to set up a computer system to keep track of health and birth certificates. With this system in place, homeless children will only have to produce these records once per school year.

Source: From *Broken Lives: Denial of Education to Homeless Children*, a report by the National Coalition for the Homeless, New York, December 1987. pp. 17–19.

HIV Illness and the Homeless

Homeless people with AIDS are predicted to become a more familiar group of the general population as the virus spreads to represent a problem of poverty. People who are already ill can lose jobs and then housing; people who are homeless can be diagnosed with the virus. Congregate shelters actually represent a health threat to HIV-

infected people, and the following reading puts forward a number
of problems these people face.

Section II. Homeless Persons with HIV Infection

The increasing number of homeless persons with HIV infection—and
homelessness in general—is a serious problem for which there are few
simple solutions. Estimates of the size of America's total homeless
population vary widely, from 400,000 (National Bureau of Economic
Research) to three million (National Coalition for the Homeless).
Reasons for homelessness also vary, but common causes include rising
housing costs, falling wages, cuts in services to the mentally ill, and,
most significantly for persons with HIV infection, discrimination.

In general, the homeless in America can be divided into three
groups, all vulnerable to the spread of the HIV epidemic. Approximately
40 percent are chronically and severely mentally ill, receive no treatment
while they live on the streets, and are subject to total health care
deprivation, multiple infections, alcohol and drug addiction, and
physical abuse. The fastest growing segment are poor families, whose
principal wage earner has become jobless or has low-paying work. These
families now account for one-third of the homeless population. The
largest homeless group is comprised of single men, of whom
approximately 30 percent are veterans. Many have been on the streets for
several years, have become desocialized, and have drug habits or criminal
histories. These are all difficult populations to reach, and persons with
HIV infection in each of these groups require a stable environment in
which to live, access to medical care, and education about transmission.

Two types of housing for homeless persons with HIV infection
currently exist and both are in critically short supply: temporary
overnight shelters and congregate living facilities that provide a
permanent residence. An increasing number of HIV-infected persons stay
in municipal shelters on a night-to-night basis and are required to leave
during the day. For these persons in particular, access to medical care is
almost non-existent. Individuals often hide their illness because discovery
may mean physical and psychological abuse, or because once diagnosed,
they are no longer eligible for shelter residency. In many instances, once
admitted to a hospital, a homeless person cannot be released until he has
a permanent address, and shelters do not qualify as official residences.
Testimony before the Commission indicated that too often homeless
persons with AIDS and HIV-related diseases die in the streets, having
found the health care system too difficult to enter or too unresponsive to
their special needs.

Persons with HIV infection may become homeless when job
discrimination or the debilitating effects of the disease result in inability
to work and inability to continue paying medical insurance premiums,
medical bills, or rent. Witnesses before the Commission have told of

being unable to obtain rental assistance and being abruptly evicted by landlords, primary tenants, or, in some instances, relatives and roommates. Testimony stated that one woman had returned from a stay in the hospital only to find herself locked out of her apartment and her belongings on the sidewalk. Housing for homeless persons with symptomatic HIV infection is even more limited than for the general homeless population. The person with HIV infection and a damaged immune system cannot survive for very long living on streets, in subways, or city parks. Even in shelters, he or she may be exposed to infectious diseases that could prove life-threatening. Among the general New York City shelter population, for example, tuberculosis has risen at an alarming rate. The housing prospects for homeless HIV-infected women with children are even more bleak.

Adolescents who live on the streets are another homeless problem directly tied to the spread of the HIV epidemic. Many of these children work on the streets as prostitutes in order to pay for food or to support a drug addiction. Organizations that assist runaway youth provide much needed protection for these adolescents, but the problem is greater than the supply of help, and prevention messages are often too late. Dr. James T. Kennedy, Medical Director of Covenant House in New York, testified before the Commission that in a recent study of his adolescent clients, 40 percent were already HIV-infected.

The housing crisis for homeless persons with symptomatic HIV infection is greatest in our large cities, which are unable to deal with their general homeless population, and are unprepared, in terms of resources, to respond to the new problem of homeless persons with HIV-related diseases. While it is difficult to establish concrete estimates of the size of the population of homeless persons with HIV, one study estimated that as many as 1,000 to 2,000 HIV-infected people reside nightly in New York City shelters. Mr. Peter Smith, President of the Partnership for the Homeless, Inc., testified before the Commission that: New York City has no separate emergency housing shelter facilities for persons with HIV-related illnesses; the rental assistance program is inadequate; only 18 scatter-site apartments are now available for persons with AIDS; the only specialized homeless facility for persons with HIV-related illnesses, Bailey House, has 44 units; and plans for renovating city-owned abandoned buildings have not been pursued.

The Commission reviewed federal housing and medical programs for the homeless and found the following obstacles to progress:

An accurate estimate of the size of the homeless population of persons with HIV infection is lacking.

Seroprevalence studies have not been done on this difficult-to-track population. An adequate assessment of the size and scope of the problem of homelessness of persons with HIV infection is necessary to target future resources.

Individuals with HIV infection may receive low priority ratings for housing subsidies due to local regulations.

Construction of shelters or group residences for persons with symptomatic HIV infection has not kept pace with demand in many cities.

Municipal shelters are unable to diagnose HIV infection or target medical resources to HIV-infected persons in shelters.

Hospitals are often unable to discharge medically stable homeless patients because they have no permanent street address.

Service needs of special populations, such as adolescents and women with children, have not been defined or estimated.

Recommendations

Federal anti-discrimination protection for persons with disabilities, including persons with HIV infection, should be expanded to cover housing that does not receive federal funds. The Department of Housing and Urban Development (HUD) should clarify that Section 504 of the Rehabilitation Act currently prohibits discrimination against persons with HIV infection if federal funds are involved. HUD should actively enforce Section 504.

The Department of Housing and Urban Development funding for homeless assistance programs should be increased, and funds should be made more easily available to cities and private sector organizations to build both temporary shelters and permanent residences for homeless persons with HIV infection.

Operators of all homeless shelters and residences must treat those clients who are HIV-infected in an anti-discriminatory manner, protect them from abuse, and help them seek medical assistance as needed.

The Centers for Disease Control should fund and coordinate targeted seroprevalence studies (e.g., on adolescents, women, and adult men) to be conducted by city agencies in high prevalence cities to establish the size of the homeless population of persons with symptomatic HIV infection and to help cities determine the need for services. In addition to HIV antibody status, these studies should gather information on concurrent medical problems, such as tuberculosis and drug addiction, to both collect co-factor information, and determine the need for greater medical intervention in municipal shelters. Study results including geographic breakdowns should be made available to national mayors' associations, to the Association of State and Territorial Health Officials, and to state and local officials, as appropriate.

The joint project between the National Institute of Mental Health and the Health Resources and Services Administration on adolescent homeless youth and HIV infection should be expanded and funding increased. More programs on homeless youth should be funded.

The Department of Housing and Urban Development should provide renovation grants to public hospitals to convert underutilized acute care beds into long-term care beds for HIV-infected individuals requiring hospice or other long-term care.

The use of the Department of Housing and Urban Development funds to help finance construction and improvement of nursing, homeless and related facilities should be encouraged to make additional long-term care and hospice care beds available.

The Veterans' Administration should conduct a short-term study to determine the extent of homelessness among veterans, and HIV infection in this population. The results of this study should be forwarded to the Secretaries of Housing and Urban Development and Health and Human Services for future resource allocation.

Source: *Report of the Presidential Commission on the Human Immunodeficiency Virus Epidemic,* 1988. pp. 104–107.

Housing and the Homeless

For any group of the homeless, a stable and permanent residence is the base from which other needs can be addressed. As the following well-documented article makes clear, affordable, decent housing is well out of the reach of someone who has experienced impoverishment as severe as homelessness.

Executive Summary

In February 1989, the U.S. Bureau of the Census and the U.S. Department of Housing and Urban Development (HUD) issued the first comprehensive set of data in more than four years on housing conditions nationwide. These data, collected as part of the American Housing Survey for 1985, show that most poor households in the United States pay extremely large portions of their limited incomes for housing costs. Using standards established by HUD, housing is considered affordable for a low income household if it consumes no more than 30 percent of the household's income. Yet the data released reveal that five of every six poor renter households paid more than 30 percent of income for housing in 1985. The new data show:

- Some 45 percent—nearly half—of all poor renter households in the nation paid at least 70 percent of income for housing, or more than the amount considered affordable under the federal standards.

- Two of every three poor renter households paid at least 50 percent of income for housing.

- Some *85 percent of poor renter households*—or 5.8 million such households—paid at least 30 percent of income for housing, or more than the amount considered affordable under the federal standards.

- The typical (or median) poor renter household had an income of less than $5,000 in 1985 (equivalent to about $5,500 in 1988) and spent 65 percent of its income on housing. Poor homeowners are nearly as hard-pressed as poor renters.

- Nearly one-third of all poor homeowners—31 percent—paid at least 70 percent of their incomes for housing in 1985.

- Nearly half paid at least 50 percent of their income on housing, while 73 percent paid at least 30 percent of income on housing.

- Poor homeowners faced high costs for housing expenses other than just their mortgage payments. The typical poor homeowner household that incurred these costs paid 35 percent of its income for fuels, other utilities, real estate taxes and insurance.

- The typical poor homeowner household—like the typical poor renter household—had an income of less than $5,000 a year. It paid 47 percent of its income for housing.

These extremely high housing costs represented a substantial burden for the 13.3 million households living below the poverty line in 1985. (The poverty level was $8,573 for a family of three in 1985.)

About three-fifths of these poor households were renters, while about two-fifths were homeowners. Approximately 60 percent were white, 25 percent were black, and 10 percent were Hispanic.

It should be noted that the American Housing Survey data on which this report is based do *not* cover most of those households who are homeless. As a result, this report provides a conservative estimate of housing problems facing poor households.

Increases in Housing Burdens Since the 1970s

The problems faced by poor households in finding affordable housing have worsened appreciably since the 1970s.

- The proportion of poor renter households who spent 60 percent or more of their income for housing grew from 44 percent in 1978 to 55 percent in 1985, an increase of 1.4 million households.

- Poor homeowners faced similar increases in housing cost burdens. In 1978, some 31 percent of poor homeowners spent at least 60 percent of their incomes for housing expenses, but by

1985 some 38 percent of poor homeowners had housing costs of this magnitude. This represents an increase of 750,000 households.

A revealing way to examine affordability problems faced by low income households is to compare the number of households with low incomes to the number of low rent units in the housing stock.

- In 1970, the number of rental units that rented for no more than 30 percent of the income of a household earning $10,000 a year (i.e., for no more than $250 a month) was approximately 2.4 million greater than the number of renter households with incomes at or below this level. (All figures for incomes and rents for years prior to 1985 are adjusted for inflation to be comparable to 1985 dollars.)

- In 1985, by contrast, there were nearly 3.7 million fewer units renting for no more than $250 a month than there were households with incomes at or below $10,000.

- Some 11.6 million renter households in 1985 had incomes of $10,000 or less, but only 7.9 million units rented for $250 a month or less. These data reflect a sharp change in the low income housing market since the 1970s.

- Moreover, the low income housing shortage was substantially more severe by 1985 than these numbers would indicate. First, some 800,000 of the 7.9 million units renting for $250 or less were vacant in 1985. They were vacant in part because they had structural deficiencies or were located in areas not considered habitable and in part because of normal turnover in rental housing markets. Second, these low rent units were not restricted to poor tenants—and nearly one-third of the occupied low rent units were occupied by renters who were not low income households.

The shortage of affordable housing was most severe for those who were the poorest: renter households with incomes below $5,000 a year.

- Some 5.4 million renter households in 1985 had incomes this low. For housing to have consumed no more than 30 percent of the incomes of these households, it would need to have rented for no more than $125 per month.

- Yet while there were 5.4 million households with incomes this low, only 2.1 million rental units had monthly costs of $125 or less.

The high housing costs borne by poor households stands in sharp contrast to the housing burdens of more affluent households.

- While 63 percent of poor renters paid more than half their income for housing, only eight percent of non-poor renters paid that much. Similarly, while 46 percent of poor homeowners paid more than half of their income for housing, just four percent of non-poor homeowners paid at this level.

- The data show quite clearly that as income rises, the portion of income spent on housing declines. While the typical household with income of less than $5,000 paid at least 69 percent of its income for rent in 1985, the typical household with an income of $20,000 to $25,000 spent 19 percent of its income for housing, and the typical household in the $40,000 to $60,000 range spent 14 percent of income for housing.

Factors Contributing to the Affordable Housing Squeeze

The increase in the shortage of low-rent housing since 1978 can be attributed primarily to a sharp increase in the numbers of poor families, a decline in the average incomes of poor families, a substantial reduction in the number of low rent units in the housing stock, and a resulting increase in rental charges.

- Between 1978 and 1985, the number of poor households rose 25 percent, from 10.5 million households in 1978 to 13.3 million in 1985.

In addition, those who are poor have grown poorer. In 1978, the typical poor family had an income that fell $3,362 below the poverty line. By 1985, the typical poor family's income fell $3,999 below the poverty line—further below than in any year since 1959, when such data were first collected. While the number of poor households has increased, the number of units renting for $250 or less (30 percent of a household's income at the $10,000 income level) has declined. There were 9.7 million such units in 1970, but only 7.9 million in 1985. This represents a loss of 1.8 million low-rent units from the housing stock, a 19 percent decline. A growing number of poor households competing for a shrinking number of low-cost units has contributed to increasing housing costs for the poor.

- In 1978, the typical poor renter household spent $229 a month for rent and utilities (in 1985 dollars).

- By 1985, the typical poor renter paid $226 a month for housing, an increase of 16 percent, after adjusting for inflation.

Large declines in household incomes and increases in housing costs have driven housing out of the affordable range for many low income households.

Substandard and Overcrowded Housing

Not only do the poor pay much higher proportions of income for housing than the non-poor, but they are also more likely to live in housing with moderate or even severe physical problems. Some 2.7 million poor households lived in substandard housing in 1985.

- More than one of every five poor renters—and one in every six poor homeowner households—lived in housing that HUD classified as having physical deficiencies.

By contrast, one in ten non-poor renters—and fewer than one in 20 non-poor homeowners—lived in housing units with deficiencies.

- Similarly, while poor households constituted 15 percent of all households, they occupied 39 percent of the units with signs of rats, 46 percent of those with holes in the floor, 32 percent of those with cracks in the walls, 29 percent of those with exposed wiring, and 31 percent of those with peeling paint.

Poor households are more than three times as likely as non-poor households to live in overcrowded conditions. (A housing unit is considered overcrowded if it houses more than one person per room.)

- In 1985, some 7.5 percent of poor households lived in overcrowded conditions, compared with two percent of households that were not poor.

- Among poor renters, one in eleven (nine percent) lived in overcrowded quarters, while 3.2 percent of non-poor renters lived in such conditions.

A large majority of low income households that live in substandard or overcrowded conditions also pay large proportions of their incomes for the inadequate housing they occupy.

Gaps in Government Assistance

For most poor households overburdened by high housing costs, government assistance through subsidized housing programs is not available. Fewer than one in three poor renter households (29 percent) received any kind of federal, state or local rent subsidy or lived in public housing in 1987.

Unlike other "safety net" programs, the poor are not legally "entitled" to housing assistance even if they meet all eligibility criteria. Rather, the number of households served each year is determined by the level of funding appropriated by the Congress. Applicants for housing assistance are often placed on waiting lists and must often wait several years before getting assistance. Many localities have closed their waiting lists because requests for assistance from eligible low income households so far outruns [*sic*] the available supply.

The 1980s have witnessed a declining federal commitment to assist poor households with their housing needs. As noted, the number of low income renter households has increased markedly over the past decade, while the number of low rent units in the private market has declined. As a result, the number of households assisted through government housing programs must rise substantially each year just to keep the shortage of affordable housing from growing larger.

- From fiscal year 1977 through fiscal year 1980, HUD made commitments to provide federal rental assistance to an average of 316,000 additional households per year. From fiscal year 1981 through fiscal year 1988, however, the number of housing commitments to serve additional households dropped sharply, to an average of 82,000 per year. The number of additional low income renters being provided housing assistance each year fell by nearly three-fourths.

- Retrenchment also occurred in the number of new households assisted each year through the rural housing programs of the Farmers Home Administration.

- Had the number of units added to the subsidized housing stock in the 1980s continued at the rate as in the late 1970s, some 1.8 million more low income households would be receiving housing assistance than are currently served.

The steep decline in new housing commitments in the 1980s—coming at a time of substantial growth in the number of poor households, and of substantial decline in the privately owned stock of low rent housing—has led to a large increase in the number of poor households that *do not* receive any housing assistance.

- In 1979, some four million poor renter households received no housing assistance.

- By 1987, this number had grown to 5.4 million, an increase of more than one third.

In contrast to the decline in the federal commitment to low income housing assistance, there has been a substantial increase in a form of federal housing assistance that primarily benefits middle and upper income families. Each year the federal government provides billions of dollars in benefits to homeowners by allowing deductions—primarily for mortgage interest payments and property taxes—from the amount of income that is taxable by the federal government. Such subsidies that result from tax deductions, credits or other tax breaks are called "tax expenditures."

- In fiscal year 1988, direct spending on federal low income housing assistance programs was $13.9 billion. In that same year, federal tax expenditures for housing totalled $53.9 billion.

- In fact, the amount of federal housing tax expenditures in just the past two fiscal years ($107.4 billion) is approximately equal to the amount of money spent directly on all low income subsidized housing programs during the 1980s ($107.7 billion).

As a result, federal housing subsidies are strongly tilted toward those who are already most affluent. The number of households with incomes below $10,000 a year is nearly the same as the number of households with incomes over $50,000 a year. Yet, the total amount of federal subsidies (from both subsidized housing programs and tax benefits) going to the higher income group is more than three times the amount going to the lower income group.

Future Trends for Subsidized Housing

Most national analysts forecast that the gap between the number of low income households and the number of units affordable by these households will grow substantially larger in the years ahead.

One of the reasons for the anticipated sharp growth in the shortage of low income housing is that many of the commitments under existing federal low income housing programs are scheduled to expire in the years ahead. Under one set of programs—Section 8 certificates and vouchers—private owners enter into contracts with a government housing agency to make their units available to low income tenants for a specified time period (usually five or 15 years), with the federal government paying that portion of the rent that exceeds 330 percent of a poor household's income.

- In the next five years, contracts covering nearly one million such units—almost one-fourth of all federally-assisted rental units—will expire. If these contracts are not renewed or continued in some form, owners will have the option of raising rents and converting the units to occupancy by a higher income clientele, converting the units to condominiums or shifting them to non-housing uses.

Under another set of federal housing programs, the federal government has been providing mortgage subsidies to private developers who in turn agree to lease their units to low and moderate income tenants for 40 years.

Developers participating in this program have the option to "pre-pay" their mortgage after 20 years and thereby free themselves of any further obligations to rent their units to low income households. For many of these units, the 20-year period is nearly up. A large number of such units are likely to be converted to housing for people at higher income levels, unless action is taken to prevent this from occurring.

- The National Low Income Housing Preservation Commission estimates that 66 percent of the subsidized housing that is provided under these programs and is eligible for prepayment— some 243,000 units—could be removed from the subsidized housing stock if no governmental action is taken.

Finally, the federal subsidy levels provided for many public and privately owned subsidized units appear not to have been adequate to maintain the units in decent condition. Many units are in disrepair and in need of maintenance or rehabilitation.

- A major study of the renovation needs of public housing units, conducted under contract with HUD, found that more than half of public housing households now live in projects needing moderate to substantial rehabilitation just to meet HUD's mandatory quality standards. The study estimated that the total costs for meeting just the backlog of major capital repairs would exceed $20 billion.

- The federal funding provided for such repairs totalled just $1.6 billion in fiscal year 1989. The Bush Administration has proposed to reduce this funding level by more than one-third, to $1 billion in fiscal year 1990.

Characteristics of Poor Households

Most poor households have very low incomes, consist of three or fewer people, and are white. However, black and Hispanic households are far more likely to be poor than are white households.

The poverty line for a family of three in 1985 was $8,573. Yet in 1985, more than three-fifths of all poor households (61 percent) had incomes below $5,000. Poor households were relatively small in size: nearly three of four poor households had three or fewer people. Overall, more than half of all poor households were headed by a woman, many by a single elderly woman living alone.

Poor renters and poor homeowners differed from each other in a number of ways. Poor homeowner households were more likely to be headed by an elderly person, to have no children and to be married. The typical head of a poor homeowner household was aged 62. In contrast, poor renter households were more likely to be younger, to have children and to be headed by a single parent (although female-headed households of two or more persons constituted only a little more than one-third of all poor renter households.) The typical head of a poor renter household was aged 38.

Of the 13.3 million poor households in 1985, some 8.1 million—or 61 percent—were white. While whites comprised a majority of poor households, blacks and Hispanics accounted for a highly disproportionate share of these households.

- Blacks comprised 11 percent of all households, but 26 percent of poor households. Similarly, Hispanics comprised six percent of all households, but 11 percent of poor households.

Housing Problems of Black and Hispanic Households

Black and Hispanic households face particularly severe housing problems. They are more likely to have excessive housing cost burdens and to live in crowded or substandard housing than are white households.

- In 1985, some 42 percent of all black households (including poor and non-poor), and 42 percent of all Hispanic households spent at least 30 percent of their income for housing. In contrast, some 27 percent of all white households had housing costs of this magnitude.

The high housing cost burdens of black and Hispanic households reflect, in part, the fact that blacks and Hispanics are more likely to have low income than whites.

- More than one of every three black households (35 percent) was poor in 1985, were more [sic] than one in every four Hispanic households (28 percent). Among white households, one in nine (11 percent) was poor in 1985.

Because poor households generally spend a greater proportion of their income on housing than do non-poor households, and because black and Hispanic households are more likely than white households to be poor, they are also more likely to bear high housing cost burdens.

While blacks and Hispanics in general bear significantly higher housing cost burdens than do whites, housing cost burdens for *poor* whites are as severe as the housing burdens borne by poor blacks and Hispanics. In fact, the proportion of poor white households with housing costs in excess of 30 percent of income actually *exceeds* the proportion of poor black and Hispanic households with housing costs of this magnitude. While 77 percent of poor black households and 79 percent of poor Hispanic households paid more than 30 percent of income for housing in 1985, some 82 percent of poor white households bore housing costs this high. However, because black and Hispanic households are more than twice as likely to be poor as white households, they are more likely to face the high housing costs associated with poverty.

Blacks and Hispanics are less likely to own their own homes than are whites. While black and Hispanic households are typically renters, white households are typically homeowners.

- In 1985, some 40 percent of all Hispanic households, and 44 percent of all black households, were homeowners. More than two-thirds of all white households—68 percent—owned their homes.

- In fact, the proportion of *poor* white households that own their own homes—46 percent—is greater than the proportion of *all* black and Hispanic households that are homeowners.

In addition to bearing high housing cost burdens, blacks and Hispanics are also more likely than whites to live in housing that is substandard or overcrowded.

- Blacks and Hispanics constituted 17 percent of all households in 1985, but 42 percent of the households living in substandard conditions.

Poor black and Hispanic households were more than twice as likely as poor white households to live in substandard housing.

- Some 33 percent of poor black households, and 27 percent of poor Hispanic households, lived in substandard housing in 1985. In contrast, 14 percent of poor white households lived in such conditions.

- In fact, the proportions of *non-poor* black and Hispanic households living in substandard conditions was greater than the proportion of *poor* white households living in such conditions.

Poor blacks and Hispanics are also more likely to live in overcrowded conditions than are poor white households. More than one in six poor Hispanic households lived in overcrowded conditions in 1985, as did one in nine poor black households. In comparison, fewer than one in twenty poor white households lived in such conditions.

Housing Problems of the Elderly and Young Families

Elderly households, including poor elderly households, are more likely to be homeowners and to have paid off their mortgages than households that are not elderly. In 1985, 74 percent of elderly households were homeowners. By comparison, some 61 percent of non-elderly households owned their homes.

The differences in rates of homeownership are even greater among poor elderly and non-elderly households. Nearly six of ten poor elderly households (57 percent) were homeowners in 1985. In contrast, only 30 percent of poor non-elderly households owned their own homes.

Despite these rates of homeownership, many elderly households that are poor bear high housing costs. Nearly three of four poor elderly households spent at least 30 percent of their income on housing in 1985, thereby exceeding the federal affordability standard. In contrast, one of four elderly households that are *not* poor had housing costs of this magnitude.

It should be noted that poor elderly households typically have lower housing cost burdens than poor households that are not elderly. In part, this reflects the higher rate of homeownership, and ownership free of mortgage payments, of poor elderly households relative to poor non-elderly households.

While the elderly poor bear lower housing costs than the non-elderly poor, the housing cost burdens of the entire elderly population—including both the poor and the non-poor—substantially exceed the housing cost burdens of the non-elderly population.

- In 1985, three out of five elderly renters (61 percent) spent at least 30 percent of their income on housing, compared with two of five non-elderly renters (44 percent).

- One of four elderly homeowners paid at least 30 percent of their income for housing, compared with one of five non-elderly homeowners.

This is due, in significant part, to the large proportion of the elderly population with relatively low incomes. About half of all elderly households had income below twice the poverty line in 1985. (Twice the poverty line equalled $10,312 for an elderly person living alone.) Fewer than one-third of non-elderly households had an income of less than twice the poverty line.

Young Single-Parent Families

According to a recent study prepared by the Joint Center for Housing Studies of Harvard University, single-parent families where the head is under 25 years of age face particularly serious housing problems.

- In 1974, the typical young single-parent renter household spent 46 percent of its income for housing. By 1987, the housing cost burden for this household family [*sic*] had grown to 81 percent of income. Moreover, in 1987, nearly one in four young single-parent families lived in substandard housing conditions.

- In large part these conditions reflect the low—and declining—incomes of young single-parent households. In 1987, the typical young single-parent household had an income of $4,859, which represents a drop of 36 percent, after adjusting for inflation, since 1974.

The same study also reveals that the housing cost burdens of *all* young households—including single-parent families, married young couple families, and single individuals—have risen more in recent years than have the housing burdens of any other age group.

For most low income households, housing has become an increasingly unaffordable commodity. With nearly two of three poor renters and nearly half of all poor homeowners paying more than 50 percent of income for housing—and with substantial numbers paying more than 70 percent of income for housing—little money remains for other necessities. These high housing cost burdens have serious implications. The severe low income housing shortage is likely to have contributed substantially to the growing problem of homelessness. In addition, these housing cost burdens are likely to have intensified other problems such as the incidence of hunger. The likelihood that a poor household will be without adequate food for part of a month is considerably greater when the household's rent consumes so much of its income that too little money is left to buy food to last through the month.

The future now looks ominous for affordable housing. The data on national trends and housing conditions suggest that just as the affordable housing problems worsened dramatically for low income households between the mid-1970s and the mid-1980s, so too are they likely to deteriorate further in the years ahead unless major changes are made in government policies and in the actions of the private sector.

Source: From *A Place To Call Home: The Crisis in Housing for the Poor.* Paul A. Leonard, Cushing N. Dolbeare, Edward B. Lazere. Center on Budget and Policy Priorities and Low Income Housing Information Service. 1989. pp. xi–xxiii.

5

Federal Legislation

AS NATIONAL AWARENESS ABOUT HOMELESSNESS increased during the 1980s, the U.S. Congress was often on the scene: conducting hearings, visiting shelters, examining the particular aspects of the problem that interested them. It was natural—given the deep cuts in the federal assisted housing budget—to turn to Congress for help. The following summary examines federal legislative efforts to assist the homeless, ranging from fine-tuning of existing programs to the only significant package of emergency aid to emerge, the McKinney Act.

Emergency Jobs Appropriations Act of 1983 (PL 98-8)

Shortly after the first congressional hearings since the Great Depression on homelessness, Congress appropriated $100 million in emergency food and shelter funds to be spent through the Federal Emergency Management Agency (FEMA). This agency was ordinarily responsible for planning for disasters, and homeless advocates did not anticipate that its record would be very good in disbursing funds for the homeless.

A national board of voluntary organizations dispensed half the funds, and the remaining monies were disbursed as formula grants to the states. Also under this act, the U.S. Department of Agriculture received $125 million for a surplus food commodities effort, the Temporary Emergency Food Assistance Program (TEFAP). Some $75 million was to purchase surplus foods and $50 million was to be used to distribute commodities.

Department of Defense Authorization Act of 1984 (PL 98-94)

Military installations could be used as shelters under this legislation.

Additional FEMA Appropriations, 1984 (PL 98-151, 98-181, 98-396)

Several 1984 appropriations measures provided an extra $110 million for distribution by FEMA. Although PL 98-181 also provided $60 million for distribution by the U.S. Department of Housing and Urban Development (HUD) for emergency shelter, the money was not disbursed because HUD claimed existing funds under the Community Development Block Grants program were being used for this purpose.

Domestic Volunteer Service Act Amendments of 1983 (PL 98-288)

Volunteers in Service to America (VISTA), the federal volunteer program, was authorized to provide its workers to homeless-related projects.

Additional FEMA Appropriations, 1985 (PL 99-98, 99-160)

FEMA was allocated $90 million for emergency food and shelter in these two appropriations.

Health Professions Training and Assistance Act of 1985 (PL 99-129)

By direction of the secretary of Health and Human Services (HHS), the National Academy of Sciences was to undertake an Institute of Medicine study of the delivery of health care services to homeless people. This study, released in late 1988 as *Homelessness, Health, and Human Needs,* was controversial because 10 of the 13 experts who wrote the report issued a supplemental opinion to the final version. The 10 felt the official report was too limited in its view of the broader problem of homelessness; they emphasized the human cost of the crisis and their position that the most basic health problem is a lack of housing.

Military Construction Authorization Act of 1986 (PL 99-167)

Using this law, military installations could make surplus bedding available to shelters for the homeless.

Food Security Act of 1985 (PL 99-198)

The TEFAP program was reauthorized by this law, with $50 million authorized per year through fiscal year 1987. However, a cost-sharing requirement was also attached, making state-level distribution efforts liable for part of the expense of the program. The law also required state welfare offices to find ways to provide food stamps to people who did not have permanent addresses.

Anti-Drug Abuse Act of 1986 (PL 99-570)

Attached to this statute was the Homeless Eligibility Clarification Act, which removed barriers faced by homeless people trying to obtain food stamps and allowed them to use food stamps to purchase prepared meals from soup kitchens and shelters. The law also required other federal agencies administering such programs as Aid to Families with Dependent Children (AFDC), Medicaid, and Supplemental Security Income (SSI) to examine eligibility barriers faced by homeless people seeking to use these programs. Further, the act banned the denial of veterans' benefits in cases in which the applicant lacked a mailing address.

The Social Security Administration (SSA) was required to make site visits to take applications at homeless facilities for SSI and food stamps. SSA and the U.S. Department of Agriculture (USDA) were also required to take applications for their programs from persons about to be discharged from hospitals, prisons, or other institutions. Finally, homeless people were made eligible for job training programs at the state and local levels that were authorized by the Job Corps Partnership Act.

Additional FEMA Appropriations, 1986 (PL 99-591)

FEMA received an additional $70 million for emergency food and shelter programs. HUD received $15 million for the Homeless Housing Act, to finance two demonstration projects, one in transitional housing and one in emergency shelter.

Omnibus Health Care Act, 1986 (PL 99-660)

The National Institute of Mental Health (NIMH) was authorized to make grants for demonstration projects for the homeless mentally ill.

Additional Appropriations, 1987 (PL 100-6)

Almost simultaneously with the introduction of Urgent Relief for the Homeless (HR 558), which became the McKinney Act, Congress made available additional funds for the rapidly approaching winter. H.J. Res. 102 was a supplemental appropriations measure that put an additional $45 million into shelter spending and $5 million into services for homeless, mentally ill veterans. This $50 million was reallocated from traditional disaster relief funds to homeless programs.

Stewart B. McKinney Homeless Assistance Act, 1987 (PL 100-77)

Proportionately more attention is devoted to the McKinney Act because it has been the major federal legislative involvement in the problem of homelessness. The act was originally introduced as HR 558, the Urgent Relief for the Homeless Act, and was subsequently named for the late Representative Stewart B. McKinney (R-CT), one of its chief proponents.

The 1987 passage of the McKinney Act was a landmark recognition by the federal government of the problem at its doorstep. There continues to be a need for temporary relief in the form of shelter, food, and support services, including the provision of medical and mental health care for homeless individuals and families.

However, this legislative response, focused as it is on short-term efforts, is inadequate as a total solution. A comprehensive effort is needed to relieve and eliminate a problem no longer confined to city streets but easily found in suburban and rural communities as well. Affirmative steps can stem the forces contributing to homelessness and put into place long-range programs that offer enduring solutions.

After years of inaction in the face of a growing crisis, the Congress approved comprehensive federal legislation to provide emergency aid to the nation's homeless poor in early 1987. Passed by overwhelming bipartisan majorities, the McKinney Act authorized just over $1 billion to be spent in 1987 and 1988.

On July 22, 1987, President Reagan reluctantly signed the bill into law. According to the White House, the president signed the McKinney Act in the evening to demonstrate his "lack of enthusiasm" for the measure (Robert Pear, "President Signs $1 Billion Bill in Homeless Aid," New York Times, 24 July 1987, A1).

The McKinney Act contains several emergency provisions, as well as a smattering of "preventive" and "transitional" programs. McKinney preventive measures, for instance, will help stave off eviction or utility cutoffs, but this only prevents an acute event within a chronic circumstance—poverty. True preventive measures would ensure that housing was decent and permanently affordable and that wages and/or benefits were sufficient to keep an individual or household from perpetually living on the edge.

The McKinney Act contains many important provisions that are discussed below.

Title I. General Provisions

General Definition of Homeless Person

A person who
(1) lacks a fixed, regular, and adequate nighttime residence, or (2) lives in:
   (a) a shelter,
   (b) an institution other than a prison, or
   (c) a place not designed for or ordinarily used as a sleeping accommodation for human beings.

Purpose

To meet the critically urgent needs of the nation's homeless, with special emphasis on elderly persons, handicapped persons, families with children, Native Americans, and veterans.

Title II. Interagency Council on the Homeless

General

This section establishes an independent entity in the executive branch as a successor to the Federal Task Force on the Homeless, which was terminated. The council consists of ten Cabinet secretaries—Agriculture, Commerce, Defense, Education, Energy, Health and Human Services, Housing and Urban Development, Interior, Labor, and Transportation—and the heads of five independent agencies—ACTION, Federal Emergency Management Agency (FEMA), General Services Administration (GSA), Department of Veterans Affairs (VA), and the Postmaster General. Jack F. Kemp, secretary of the Department of Housing and Urban Development, is the chair and Patricia Carlile is the executive director of the council.

Bimonthly Bulletin

The council must distribute a bimonthly bulletin to states, local governments, and public and private nonprofits on federal resources available under the McKinney Act, including application deadlines and federal agency contact persons. The bulletin is called "Council Communiqué."

Duties of the Council

(1) Review federal activities and programs;
(2) Reduce duplication among federal programs;
(3) Monitor and evaluate federal, state, local, and private programs and activities;

(4) Provide technical assistance to state, local, and private groups;

(5) Collect and disseminate information; and

(6) Employ at least two, but no more than five, regional coordinators to:

    (a) coordinate the council's activities within the ten standard federal regions;

    (b) interpret federal regulations;

    (c) assist in the federal application process, including grant applications;

    (d) coordinate McKinney programs with other federal programs; and

    (e) develop recommendations for regional solutions to homeless issues.

Reports

The council must prepare annual reports to Congress and the president regarding the nature and extent of homelessness; the activities of the federal government in meeting the needs of the homeless and in working with federal, state, local, and private entities; the level of federal assistance necessary; and recommendations.

State Councils and Contacts

Each state is encouraged to establish its own state Interagency Council on the Homeless and is required to designate a contact person to receive and disseminate information on homeless programs.

Title III. Emergency Food and Shelter Program

National Board

Establishes the Emergency Food and Shelter National Board, chaired by the director of the Federal Emergency Management Agency (FEMA). Members are to be nominated by six private nonprofit organizations.

Local Boards

The national board will designate ten local boards consisting primarily of representatives of the same organizations as the national board as well as the mayor or other local government head. Local boards determine how funds allocated to each locality will be distributed and also monitor recipients of funds.

Grants

The national board must disburse funds to private nonprofit organizations and local governments within three months of when funds become available:

(1) to expand ongoing efforts to provide shelter, food, and supportive services and to facilitate access to other sources of services and benefits, with special emphasis on the transition to permanent housing and the needs of mentally or physically disabled persons;

(2) to strengthen innovative local programs;

(3) to conduct minimum rehabilitation of existing mass shelters or feeding facilities, but only to the extent necessary to make them safe and sanitary.

Not more than 5 percent of the total amount appropriated each year may be used for administrative costs.

Program Guidelines

The national board must establish written guidelines, including methods for identifying localities with the highest needs and determining amounts allocated.

Title IV. Housing Assistance

A. Comprehensive Homeless Assistance Plan (CHAP)

General
States, eligible cities, and urban counties must annually submit and receive approval for a CHAP, to receive assistance above Emergency Shelter Grant minimums, for any McKinney program administered by HUD. Private applicants need not submit a plan but must be in a state with an approved plan. States must submit a copy of their comprehensive plan to metropolitan cities and urban counties; metropolitan cities and urban counties must submit a copy of their plan to their state.

Contents
Each comprehensive plan must contain:

(1) a description of the need for assistance;
(2) an inventory of existing facilities and services;
(3) a strategy to:

    (a) match needs with available services, and
    (b) recognize special needs, particularly those of families with children, the elderly, the mentally ill, and veterans;

(4) an explanation of how federal assistance will complement and enhance available services;
(5) identification of the contact person or agency that coordinates homeless assistance; and
(6) an assurance that each recipient and project sponsor shall administer, in good faith, a policy designed to ensure that the homeless facility is

free from the illegal use, possession, or distribution of drugs or alcohol.

B. Emergency Shelter Grants

General
Grants are distributed by HUD:

(1) to states for distribution to local governments, cities, counties, and private nonprofit organizations that have obtained local government certification of support for their project, and
(2) directly to cities and counties eligible for at least the minimum grant (.05 percent of the total appropriation, or $25,000 for fiscal year 1989).

Local governments may distribute all or some of their grants to private nonprofits. States, cities, and counties eligible for direct grants must obtain approval of their comprehensive plans before they can be awarded grants.

Eligible Activities
Grants may be used for:

(1) renovations, rehabilitation, or conversion of buildings to be used as emergency shelters;

(2) maintenance, operations (other than staff), insurance, utilities, and furnishings;

(3) essential services, including employment, health, and drug abuse or education services if local government has not provided such services during any part of the preceding year or if assistance under this subtitle would complement those services. Not more than 20 percent of a grant to a local government may be used for such services unless allowed by the HUD secretary. Efforts to prevent homelessness are considered essential services. Homelessness prevention assistance may be given if:

(a) the family cannot make required payments because of a sudden income reduction;

(b) the program assistance is necessary to avoid eviction or termination of services;

(c) there is a reasonable prospect that the family will be able to resume payments within a reasonable time period; and

(d) the assistance would not supplant existing assistance from other sources.

Reporting
The comptroller general must report to Congress on the various programs to prevent homelessness that are implemented by grantees. The report should focus on eligibility requirements of homelessness prevention programs and include:

(1) an examination of other federal, state, and local homelessness prevention programs; and

(2) recommendations for legislation, including recommendation for programs to prevent homelessness resulting from mortgage foreclosures.

Certification
Each grant recipient must certify that:

(1) any building for which assistance is used will be maintained as a shelter for three years or, if major rehabilitation or conversion is done, for ten years (if assistance is used only for essential services and operating expenses, the grant recipient must provide services or shelter without regard to a particular site as long as the same general population is served);

(2) any renovated buildings will be safe and sanitary;

(3) it will assist homeless persons to obtain

  (a) appropriate supportive services, and
  (b) other available government or private assistance.

C. Supportive Housing Demonstration Program

General
Establishes a demonstration program administered by HUD to develop innovative approaches for providing supportive housing, especially for deinstitutionalized persons, families, mentally ill persons, and handicapped persons. In general, states, cities, counties, tribes, private nonprofits, and public housing authorities may apply for assistance. However, only states may apply for assistance for permanent housing for handicapped homeless persons.

Definitions
Supportive housing includes:

(1) transitional housing designed to facilitate movement into independent living within 24 months, and

(2) permanent housing for handicapped persons that is community based, serves not more than eight persons, provides services, and is operated by a nonprofit sponsor.

The HUD secretary can waive the eight-person limitation if the applicant demonstrates that:

(1) local market conditions dictate the development of a larger project, and

(2) such development will achieve the neighborhood integration objective of the program within the context of the affected community.

"Supportive services" means services addressing the special needs of deinstitutionalized homeless persons, homeless families, and handicapped homeless persons.

Occupant Rent
Each homeless individual residing in supportive housing must pay rent in accordance with section 3(a) of the U.S. Housing Act of 1937.

Matching

(1) Transitional Housing
50 percent matching requirement, may include value of donated material, building or lease; and salaries paid to staff or residents, and the value of volunteer time and services;

(2) Permanent Housing
50 percent matching requirement by state and local funds which may include the same items as (1); only 50 percent of these may be local funds. The HUD secretary may waive this requirement.

D. Supplemental Assistance for Facilities to Assist the Homeless (SAFAH)

General
Establishes a program of assistance to states, cities, counties, tribes, or private nonprofits:

(1) to provide funds for costs in excess of monies supplied by the emergency shelter grant or supportive housing programs if such costs are incurred in efforts to:

   (a) meet the special needs of homeless families or elderly or handicapped homeless persons;
   (b) facilitate the use of public buildings to assist homeless persons; or
   (c) provide supportive services for the homeless.

(2) to provide comprehensive assistance to particularly innovative programs by assisting in:

   (a) the purchase, lease, renovation, operation, or conversion of facilities; or
   (b) the provision of supportive services including food, child care, assistance in obtaining permanent housing, outpatient health services, employment and nutritional counseling, and provision of security.

To the extent practical, the HUD secretary must use at least 50 percent of the funds for facilities that primarily benefit homeless elderly persons and homeless families, and must distribute funds equitably across geographic areas.

Health Care
Not more than $10,000 of any grant or advance may be used for
outpatient health services. Grants may not be used to purchase major
medical equipment.

Application
The applicant must:

(1) show commitment to alleviating poverty;
(2) furnish assurances that the project will be operated for at least ten
years;
(3) show continuing capacity to provide assistance;
(4) comply with any other requirements the HUD secretary may
establish; and
(5) provide documentation of site control.

E. Section 8 Assistance for Single Room Occupancy Units (SRO)

General
Section 8 funding is increased to provide assistance for moderate
rehabilitation of SROs for use by homeless persons. Funds may be used
for efficiency apartments if the owner pays additional rehabilitation and
operating costs.

Procedure
HUD will allocate funds to applicants that best demonstrate need and
ability to carry out a program, based on a national competition.
Applicants must submit to the HUD secretary written proposals
containing:

(1) a description of project size and characteristics of potential
occupants;
(2) a list of public and private sources of additional aid;
(3) an inventory of suitable housing stock to be rehabilitated; and
(4) a description of interest in participating shown by builders,
developers, and others.

Limitations
No city or county may receive more than 10 percent of total assistance
available. Rehabilitation costs compensated under the program may not
exceed $14,000 per unit, plus required fire and safety costs, unless the
HUD secretary determines that local conditions justify higher cost.

F. Reports

Rent Control
The HUD secretary shall submit within 12 months from November 7,
1989, a report to Congress evaluating the impact of local housing rent
control and regulations on the rate of homelessness in major U.S. cities.

Title V. Identification and Use of Unused and Underutilized Surplus Federal Property

Identification

The secretary of HUD is required to collect information about unused and underused federal property from surveys conducted by the heads of the other federal agencies. The secretary, in consultation with the Department of Health and Human Services (HHS) and the General Services Administration (GSA), must develop criteria for determining the suitability of such property for use as facilities for the homeless and must actually identify suitable property within two months of collecting the above information.

Notification

The HUD secretary must notify each federal agency of any property suitable for use for the homeless. Within 30 days of receipt of such notice, the agency must respond to HUD and GSA, stating:

(1) the property will be made available, or
(2) the reasons the property cannot be made available.

Use of Property to Assist Homeless

Once properties are deemed suitable, GSA and HHS must take the necessary action to make the properties available as homeless assistance facilities operated by states, local governments, or private nonprofits.

Leases

Property may be used only through leases lasting at least one year. Ownership shall not be transferred.

Reports

By October 20, 1987, and quarterly thereafter, GSA shall submit to Congress and the Interagency Council on the Homeless reports on implementation, including:

(1) a list of properties identified by HUD as suitable;
(2) a statement of agencies' responses to HUD notices; and
(3) a statement of actions taken by GSA and HHS to make such properties available.

The judge in the case *National Coalition for the Homeless et al. v. Veterans Administration et al.* ruled on December 15, 1988, that:

(1) HUD must survey all unused or underused surplus and excess federal property for the possible use of the homeless;

(2) HUD must list the suitable properties weekly in the *Federal Register*; and

(3) HHS must process all applications for the property.

Title VI. Health Care for the Homeless

A. Primary Health Services and Substance Abuse Services

1. Health Services for the Homeless Grant Program
Establishes a program requiring the secretary of HHS to make grants for the delivery of primary health care and substance abuse services to homeless persons including individuals residing in transitional housing.

Services
Each grantee must agree to provide, directly or through contract:

(1) health services at locations accessible to homeless persons;
(2) 24-hour emergency health services;
(3) appropriate referrals for necessary hospital services;
(4) referrals to mental health services;
(5) outreach;
(6) assistance in obtaining services under entitlement programs; and
(7) continuation of services to a formerly homeless individual, after the person has found housing, for up to 12 months.

Limitations on Charges
Each grantee must agree to provide services regardless of recipient's ability to pay. No charge may be imposed on a homeless person with income below poverty level.

Optional Provisions
Grantees, at their option, may provide mental health services, may make referrals to advocacy groups for mentally ill homeless persons, and may provide services through self-help organizations.

2. National Health Services Corporation
Amends Public Health Service Act to include homeless persons as a population with a shortage of health professionals serving it. This makes homeless persons eligible to receive a National Health Services Corporation provider.

3. Deinstitutionalization Study
By April 1989, the secretary of HHS must prepare a study determining the extent to which state deinstitutionalization policies contribute to homelessness and submit the study to Congress with any recommendations.

B. *Community Mental Health Services for the Homeless*

1. Mental Health Block Grant

General
Establishes a block grant program administered by HHS, allotting funds to states for the provision of community mental health services to chronically mentally ill homeless persons.

Required Services
Each state must agree that the project's funds will provide the following services:

(1) outreach;
(2) community mental health services;
(3) referrals to hospital services, primary health care, and substance abuse services;
(4) case management, including:

   (a) preparing a mental health services plan and reviewing it at least once every three months,
   (b) providing assistance in obtaining services and benefits,
   (c) referring the person for other services, and
   (d) providing representative payee services;

(5) supportive and supervisory services in residential settings not funded by the supportive housing program; and
(6) training of shelter and mental health clinic staff.

Items 1 through 3 may be provided to mentally ill persons who have a significant probability of becoming homeless, as well as to homeless persons.

2. Demonstration Projects for Chronically Mentally Ill Homeless Persons

General
Authorizes additional funds for the existing Community Support Program, a demonstration project administered by the National Institute of Mental Health (NIMH) to provide community-based services to chronically mentally ill persons. Additional funds are to be used only to provide such services to homeless, chronically mentally ill persons.

3. Demonstration Projects for Alcohol and Drug Abuse Treatment

General
Directs the HHS secretary to make grants to community-based public and private entities for alcohol and drug abuse treatment services for homeless persons.

Title VII. Education, Training, and Community Services Programs

A. Adult Literacy

General
The Adult Education Act is amended to make clear that homeless adults
are eligible.

Grant Program
The secretary of education may make grants to state education agencies
to develop and implement literacy training programs for homeless
persons. Programs must include outreach and coordinate with existing
services. State education agencies must submit applications to the
secretary in accordance with reasonable requirements (to be issued by the
secretary). Funds will be distributed based on assessments of homeless
populations made in the state's Comprehensive Homeless Assistance
Plans under this act.

B. Education for Homeless Children

1. Policy
Each state education agency must ensure that homeless children have
access to free and appropriate public school education and that state
residence requirements do not bar access.

2. Grant Program
General
Establishes a program of grants by the secretary of education to the states
to:

(1) carry out the above policies;
(2) establish a state office of Coordinator of Education of Homeless
Children and Youth; and
(3) prepare and carry out the state plan.

Office of Coordinator
The office of the coordinator, established in each state, annually gathers
data on the number of homeless children and the extent of their
problems in gaining access to education and also develops and carries
out the state plan. The coordinator must submit a final report by
December 31 of each year.

State Plan
Each state must adopt a plan for the education of homeless children and
establish procedures to resolve disputes regarding the educational
placement of homeless children. In addition, each plan must ensure, to
the extent practical under local education laws, that:

(1) local education authorities either continue the education of the child
in the original school district for the rest of the school year or place the

child in the district he is actually living in, whichever is in the child's best interest;

(2) each homeless child is provided the same services as other children; and

(3) the records of each homeless child who is transferred to a new school district are available in that district in a timely manner.

3. Exemplary Grants Program for Homeless Children

Establishes a program for the education secretary to make grants for exemplary programs that successfully address the needs of homeless children in school. Grants are to be made to state and local education authorities in states that have submitted a state plan. The secretary must disseminate information on exemplary programs to the state and local educational authorities.

C. Job Training

1. Job Training for the Homeless Demonstration Program

General

Establishes a program for the secretary of labor to make grants for job training demonstration projects for homeless persons. Grants may go to public agencies, private nonprofits, private businesses, and other appropriate entities.

State Coordination

The state in which projects are located must describe, as part of its comprehensive plan (see Title IV), how it will coordinate projects with other services for homeless persons that are provided for under the McKinney Act.

Activities

Eligible activities include:

(1) basic skills instruction;
(2) remedial education;
(3) basic literacy instruction;
(4) job search;
(5) job counseling; and
(6) job preparatory training (e.g., résumé writing).

2. Homeless Veterans Reintegration Project

General

Establishes a grant program for the secretary of labor to fund programs to expedite reintegration of homeless veterans into the labor force. Funds may be used for job training, remedial education, basic literacy instruction, job counseling, and outreach referrals to homeless veterans. Local agencies must apply to states.

3. Job Training Partnership Act

Amended to assist homeless persons in obtaining employment and training services.

D. Emergency Community Services Homeless Grant Program

General
Establishes a special grant program administered by the Office of Community Services of the Department of Health and Human Services (HHS). Funds are allocated to states that administer programs under the Community Services Block Grant (CSBG) program in accordance with the CSBG formula. If a state does not apply for funds, the HHS secretary will make grants directly to eligible agencies within that state.

Eligible Activities
Funds can be used only to:

(1) expand comprehensive services to homeless persons to assist in the transition out of poverty;

(2) assist in obtaining social services and benefits;

(3) promote private sector and other assistance; and

(4) assist in homelessness prevention, though only 25 percent of the funds can be used for this purpose. Funds cannot be used for state administrative costs.

E. Jobs for Employable Dependent Individuals (JEDI)

General
Establishes incentive bonuses to states for successful job placement of welfare recipients.

Eligibility
An individual can be counted if that person:

(1) has been a welfare recipient during 24 of the previous 28 months, is the head of a household, and has had no "significant" work experience during the previous year; or

(2) is presently receiving welfare, is the head of a household, is less than 22 years old, and has had no "significant" work experience during the previous year; or

(3) is blind or disabled, has received disability insurance for 24 of the previous 28 months, and has had no "significant" work experience during the previous year; or

(4) is blind or disabled, is presently receiving disability insurance, is less than 22 years old, and has had no "significant" work experience during the previous year.

Additional Requirement
The individual must have successfully participated in education,
training, or other activities offered under JEDI; be placed in non-
subsidized employment; receive income greater than or equal to bonus
base; and no longer require welfare.

Placement Bonus Base
This is equal to an annual average of the federal welfare contribution to
an individual or family during the previous two years.

Amount of Incentive Bonus
The incentive bonus given to eligible states is 75 percent of the
placement bonus base for initial placement, 75 percent of the placement
bonus base for second continuous year of employment, and 75 percent of
the placement bonus base for third continuous year of employment.
Bonuses are given for placements made in each eligible category above
the number placed in program year 1987 or any other base period agreed
to by the governor and the secretary of labor.

Duties of the Secretary
The secretary is responsible for:

(1) providing technical assistance to facilitate the collection, exchange,
and compilation of data required by the program;

(2) providing financial assistance for start-up costs to governors;

(3) establishing a performance standard for JEDI;

(4) issuing proposed regulations for JEDI not later than three months
after enactment and final rules within seven months; and

(5) evaluating the program and reporting to Congress the results of the
evaluation by January 1, 1996.

Title VIII. Veterans' Provisions

General
Provides 50 percent of funding for conversion of surplus VA space to
domiciling beds for homeless veterans and 50 percent of funding for
medical care for homeless, chronically mentally ill veterans.

Title IX. Aid to Families with Dependent Children (AFDC); Unemployment Compensation

*A. Extension on Prohibition against Implementation of Certain
Proposed Regulations*

Extends for one year (i.e., through September 30, 1989) the moratorium
on implementation of regulations restricting the scope of AFDC

emergency assistance and limiting the states' ability to use AFDC funds for temporary housing needs.

B. Report on AFDC as Emergency Assistance

Requires HHS to review the policies currently in effect, in which states use funds from Title IV-A of the Social Security Act either as AFDC payments for special needs or as emergency assistance to meet emergency needs of families who are eligible for AFDC aid. The secretary must report legislative and regulatory recommendations to:

(1) improve the AFDC program's ability to meet emergency needs of eligible families, and

(2) eliminate state use of AFDC funds for shelter in commercial or similar transient facilities by July 1, 1989.

C. Demonstration Projects to Reduce the Number of Homeless Families in Welfare Hotels

General
Authorizes two to three states to conduct demonstration projects to put AFDC families in transitional facilities instead of welfare hotels.

Project Requirements
The project must:

(1) provide transitional housing only to AFDC families in commercial or similar transient facilities;

(2) permanently reduce the number of commercial or transient rooms used for AFDC families by the same number of units made available under the demonstration; and

(3) provide that the total amount of federal payments for cash assistance to families in transitional facilities, together with federal payments under the project, shall be less than or equal to the federal cost of housing such families in commercial or transitional facilities (including payments for their basic needs and services).

Use of Funds
Funds may be used:

(1) for rehabilitation or construction of transitional facilities that can be easily converted to permanent housing, and

(2) to provide on-site social services.

6

Significant Court Cases

SOME OF THE FIRST EFFORTS to battle homelessness were in the courts, as legal advocates who witnessed growing homelessness sought to establish rights for people who had been stripped of legal existence. The following overview of cases covers a wide variety of claims made in the last decade as attorneys have tried to address both the causes and effects of the problem.

Right to Shelter

Callahan v. Carey,
N.Y.L.J. (Dec. 11, 1979) at 10, col. 4 (N.Y. Sup. Ct., Dec. 5, 1979)

This suit was filed in 1979 on behalf of four homeless men in New York City. It was the first case of its kind and resulted in an initial ruling by the state Supreme Court that the New York Constitution requires the state and city to provide shelter to the homeless. In August 1981, following complex litigation and after the city and state lost the initial legal ruling, a settlement was reached requiring the city to provide safe and decent shelter to homeless men. The Callahan case was brought with a focus on homeless men because of the significant difference in the quality and availability of shelters for the two sexes in the late 1970s.

Since that consent decree was entered, a number of proceedings have been brought both by the plaintiffs and by the city. Typically, the plaintiffs have challenged the city's non-compliance with the decree.

Orders have been secured requiring the city to open additional beds, to increase some kinds of facilities in certain shelters, and to reduce the population in others. Each fall, as shelters become more crowded, violations of the decree are challenged.

Eldredge v. Koch,
119 Misc. 2d 163, 459 N.Y.S.2d 960 (N.Y. Sup. Ct.),
rev'd in part, 98 A.D.2d 675, 469 N.Y.S.2d 744 (1st Dep't 1983)

The *Callahan* decree was to apply equally to homeless men and women, according to the city, but it soon became apparent that shelters for women did not meet the *Callahan* standards. This case affirmed that the *Callahan* decree applied to women's shelters as well.

Hodge v. Ginsberg, 303 S.E.2d 245 (W.V. 1983)

The West Virginia Supreme Court of Appeals ruled that, under protective services laws, the state must provide shelter, food, and medical care for the homeless in that state.

Maticka v. Atlantic City,
524 A.2d (N.J. Super. Ct., App. Div. 1987)

The superior court held that state protective services law guarantees a right to shelter for general assistance applicants who are homeless.

Klosterman v. Cuomo,
No. 11270/82 (N.Y. App. Div. filed May 20, 1982), on remand,
126 Misc. 2d 247, 481 N.Y.S.2d 580 (Sup. Ct. N.Y. Co. 1984)

Supportive community housing for 6,000 former state psychiatric patients who had become homeless after release was the goal of this case. New York's highest court held in 1984 that state officials should enforce the rights of the homeless mentally ill and that lack of funds was not a defense for failing to provide those rights.

Koster v. Webb, 598 F. Supp. 1134 (E.D.N.Y. 1983);
see also 108 F.R.D. 46 (E.D.N.Y. 1985)

A group of homeless families in Nassau County, New York, brought this case in late 1982, alleging that the county failed to provide them with decent emergency shelter. For the first time, the court recognized a federal claim in a case of this type, citing the families' right to shelter under the federal Social Security Act. This suit was settled in 1987, with the jurisdictions agreeing to provide shelter that meets specific standards for all homeless families.

Committee for Dignity and Fairness for the Homeless v. Pernsley, No. 886 (Pa. Ct. of Common Pleas, settled April 1985)

A right to shelter was successfully forced through local law in this case brought by homeless people in Philadelphia.

Graham et al. v. Schoemehl, No. 854-00035 (Mo. Cir. Ct., City of St. Louis, Nov. 15, 1985)

This suit on behalf of homeless people alleged that an 1815 state statute providing for the poor required St. Louis to aid its homeless. A subsequent consent decree in the case provided for shelter and services, as well as additional permanent housing.

McCain v. Koch, 117 A.D.2d 198, 502 N.Y.S.2d 720 (1st Dep't 1986); Cannady v. Koch, 608 F. Supp. 1460 (S.D.N.Y. 1985)

Homeless families in New York were guaranteed a right to emergency shelter by this suit. When the city exhausted its supply of shelters and hotel beds for homeless families in late 1984, mothers and their children were relegated to sleeping in welfare offices when city officials refused to procure other accommodations.

Palmer v. Cuomo, Index No. 2307/85 (Sup. Ct. N.Y. Co. 1985), aff'd, 121 A.D.2d 194, 503 N.Y.S.2d 20 (1st Dep't 1986)

A group of homeless young people under the age of 21 brought this suit, which successfully sought relief for young persons who were discharged from the foster care system onto the streets. The plaintiffs sought care until age 21, as well as education and training necessary for independent living. The state subsequently issued new regulations defining this responsibility.

Coker v. Bowen, Civ. No. 86-2448 (D.D.C.)

The National Coalition for the Homeless sought to force the U.S. Department of Health and Human Services to require the 25 states participating in the emergency assistance to families program to provide emergency shelter to homeless families. The case was dismissed in early 1989 and is being appealed.

Shelter Standards

Atchison v. Barry et al., Civil Action No. 88-11976
(D.C. Super. Ct. Civ. Div., Apr. 14, 1989)

This agreement settled a follow-up case to the Washington, D.C., right-to-overnight-shelter law, passed in 1984. The agreement set operating and quality standards for the five men's shelters and three women's shelters operated by the city, as well as terms for opening additional shelters around the city.

Intake Requirements

Lubetkin v. City Manager of Hartford,
No. CV-83-0280505S (Conn. Super. Ct. filed Feb. 4, 1983)

This class action case alleged that the city of Hartford's practice of requiring verification of residence before accepting or processing applications for general assistance (including shelter) violated state law.

Eisenheim v. Los Angeles Board of Supervisors,
No. C-479 453 (Cal. Super. Ct. 1984)

Homeless people in Los Angeles challenged the county's refusal to offer shelter vouchers to persons who lacked extensive identification papers. A dozen California religious figures joined a friend of the court brief, drafted by the National Coalition for the Homeless, advising the court on how this practice effectively prevents the homeless from receiving aid. Officials agreed to stop requiring identification.

Tucker v. Battistoni, No. 6297/86 (Dutchess County)

This action challenged a practice in about 50 percent of New York's upstate counties in which persons were deemed ineligible for emergency shelter if they missed a single appointment with a welfare officer. These so-called sanctions were used to deny persons shelter for up to 90 days, even when the person appeared for an appointment the following day.

Due Process

Williams v. Barry,
No. CV-80-1104 (D.C., June 8, 1982)

Washington, D.C., sought to close its only publicly sponsored shelters
for homeless men on 48 hours' notice. This suit on behalf of some shelter
residents found that, although the men had an entitlement to shelter
based on the fact that the facilities had been open more than two years
and residents had an expectation of continued services, due process
required only notice and an opportunity for the homeless men to submit
written comments before the closing took place. The plaintiffs' request
that oral hearings were more appropriate for those at risk was rejected. A
court order kept the shelters open for more than two years while the case
was pending.

Weiser v. Koch,
84 Civ. 1837 (S.D.N.Y. filed March 15, 1985)

Homeless men and women challenged New York City's practice of
evicting people from municipal shelters without following set guidelines
or procedures. An agreement was reached strictly limiting the
circumstances under which a person could be evicted.

Status Offenses

Davenport v. People of the State of California,
No. 85-6171 (Cal. Super. Ct. 1985)

Homelessness was effectively being criminalized by the enforcement of a
county statute in Santa Barbara, California, which banned sleeping in
public at night. The lower court found the ordinance unconstitutional,
but was reversed. The National Coalition for the Homeless sought to
have the U.S. Supreme Court review the convictions of homeless people
prosecuted under the ban, but the court refused.

Right to Treatment

Ruth v. Health and Hospitals Corporation,
85 Civ. 7548 (S.D.N.Y.)

This suit was filed in late 1985 to challenge the practice of municipal hospitals in New York failing to provide beds for psychiatric patients admitted to those hospitals. Mentally ill people were being forced to wait in hospital emergency rooms for as long as four days because of the shortage of beds.

Love v. Koch, No. 4514/88 (N.Y. Sup. Ct.)

This pending class action suit for mentally disabled people contends that a place to live is a component of appropriate mental health care. The suit argues that either community care, acute hospitalization, or residential treatment must be provided; outpatient treatment with a referral to a shelter is inappropriate.

Foster Care

In the Matter of P. et al., (D.C. Super. Ct. filed April 12, 1982)

After being homeless for six months because of a fire in their public housing unit, the children of this family were placed in foster care. The city would not rehouse the family because of a debt dispute. One year later, the family was still separated. A consent decree finally placed the family in housing while the city searched for a subsidized unit, and the family was reunited.

Right to Appropriate Housing

Baby Jennifer v. Koch, 86 Civ. 9676 (S.D.N.Y.)

This class action suit was brought against New York State and New York City officials on behalf of several hundred healthy infants, known as "boarder babies." The infants, most of whom had been abandoned by drug-addicted mothers, were living in hospital wards simply because officials had not found homes for them. A final consent judgment was entered mandating that the city develop sufficient foster care placements with families so that it could cease to leave infants in hospitals.

Mixon v. Grinker, No. 14392/88 (N.Y. Sup. Ct. filed July 28, 1988)

This class action suit sought medically appropriate housing—including a private sleeping accommodation and private sanitary facilities—for persons who are HIV-seropositive. Conditions in the city shelters and on the streets endanger people with AIDS, according to the suit, and placement in a shelter cannot be considered adequate.

Right to Vote

Pitts v. Black, 608 F. Supp. 696 (S.D.N.Y. 1984)

Homeless people sued the state and city boards of election to challenge their disenfranchisement, which was based on their homelessness. Because they were living in hotels, in shelters, or on the street, they were not permitted to register to vote, with officials claiming that "a place of temporary shelter cannot be deemed a residence." A consent decree was signed before trial, permitting the homeless in shelters to vote, and in October 1984, the federal court ordered election officials to allow those homeless people living on the street to register, including a provision extending the registration period by two weeks for them.

In the Matter of: The Applications for Voter Registration of Willie R. Jenkins et al., District of Columbia Board of Elections and Ethics (June 7, 1984)

While not a court case, this D.C. proceeding interpreted the residency requirement for voting in favor of homeless persons by allowing designation of a location as home, with an accompanying effective local mailing address. This challenge occurred when homeless advocates sought to register homeless voters so they would be eligible to sign and circulate petitions to put a right-to-shelter initiative on the ballot.

Prevention

Franklin v. New Jersey Department of Human Services,
No. A-213/214 (N.J. Sup. Ct., June 24, 1988)

The court upheld the state limit of five months on provision of emergency assistance to families threatened by homelessness. The court did not reject a right-to-shelter claim, but found that other programs to prevent homelessness might help such families even if they lost emergency assistance.

Jiggets v. Grinker,
139 Misc. 2d 476, 528 N.Y.S. 2d 462
(N.Y. Sup. Ct., App. Div., June 15, 1989)

The court found that the plaintiffs might succeed on their claim that state laws mandated an AFDC shelter payment sufficient to prevent homelessness and required payment of rent arrears for rent due in excess of the shelter payment maximum. The state's highest appellate court unanimously ruled in April 1990 that the social services department has a duty to provide such payments.

First Amendment Rights

Clark v. Community for Creative Non-Violence (CCNV),
703 F.2d 586 (D.C. Cir 1984)

An unusual First Amendment case involving CCNV's challenge to federal regulations prohibiting the homeless from sleeping in Lafayette Park, across from the White House, as part of a demonstration protesting federal policies that cause homelessness. In June 1984, the court upheld the regulations.

Preservation and Displacement

Lacko v. City of Chicago
No. 82-C-5031 (E.D. Ill. consent decree June 12, 1984)

A federally funded urban renewal project displaced 300 men from two residential hotels in Chicago; homeless, they were subsequently denied relocation benefits and services by the city. The city paid each man $10 if he could show that he had rented another unit. A consent decree required additional significant payments to the men, as well as a study of low-income housing opportunities in the city, including units recently demolished or converted.

Seawall Associates v. City of New York, No. 20891/86 (N.Y. 1989)

A group of New York real estate developers sued to enjoin enforcement of a city statute barring the demolition or conversion of single room occupancy (SRO) hotels and requiring that habitable units in SROs be made available for rent, a so-called anti-warehousing provision to prohibit hoarding of units in order to empty a building. A lower court held the law unconstitutional, but the New York City Coalition for the Homeless and several residents of SRO hotels intervened, and the law was upheld on appeal. The U.S. Supreme Court refused to hear the case.

Federal Programs

Community for Creative Non-Violence v. Pierce, 786 F.2d 1199 (D.C. Cir. 1986), No. 84-5632

The controversial 1984 Department of Housing and Urban Development (HUD) study of homelessness arrived at a relatively low figure for the size of the homeless population: 250,000–300,000. The Community for Creative Non-Violence (CCNV) suit alleged that the understated report was conducted in an unprofessional manner and that it would have severe consequences for future federal spending. The case was dismissed in September 1984, with the judge concluding that CCNV lacked standing for failing to show that the study would adversely affect either public or private spending for the homeless.

Bruce v. Department of Defense (DOD), Civ. Action No. 87-0425 (D.D.C. filed June 16, 1987)

In this suit, a homeless man, an emergency shelter, and the National Coalition for the Homeless sued DOD under a federal program to make unused military facilities available as emergency shelter. Congress enacted such a statute in 1983, and the plaintiffs alleged that DOD had ignored the mandate to implement the program. In June 1987, the court ordered DOD to issue regulations to implement the program by mid-November.

National Coalition for the Homeless v. Pierce,
Civ. Action No. 87-2640 (D.D.C. filed Sept. 25, 1987)

This case was the first of several filed after the 1987 passage of the Stewart B. McKinney Homeless Assistance Act in order to implement some portion of the legislation. The suit alleged that the U.S. Department of Housing and Urban Development (HUD) had failed to enforce the Supplemental Assistance to the Homeless program because HUD did not make funds available by a specified date, which was intended to ensure operation by the next winter. HUD Secretary Samuel Pierce issued necessary guidelines for the release of the funds on the morning of the scheduled court hearing.

National Coalition for the Homeless v.
Department of Education,
Civ. Action No. 87-3512 (D.D.C. Jan. 21, 1988)

This McKinney-related suit, brought by the National Coalition for the Homeless, five homeless children, and two shelters, alleged that the Department of Education (DOE) had failed to comply with the legislative requirement to implement a program ensuring homeless children access to education. The law required such measures by the fall of 1987, to conform to the upcoming school year, but the department guidelines that were challenged in this case resulted in a delay to the following spring. The DOE set an implementation deadline and agreed to monitor state participation.

National Coalition for the Homeless et al. v.
Veterans Administration et al.,
695 F.Supp. 1226 (D.D.C. 1988)

This suit was filed against five major federal landholding agencies, alleging that the agencies violated the McKinney Title V requirements to make underutilized federal government property available to states, local governments, and private nonprofit organizations for use as facilities to assist the homeless. The court issued a strongly worded opinion and ordered the federal agencies to comply with the law on a strict schedule, with properties to be available exclusively for use by the homeless during the first 30 days of their listing. HUD was further required to list such properties weekly in the *Federal Register*. After noncompliance by HHS, a motion to enforce was granted in May 1989.

Other Claims

Robbins v. Reagan,
780 F.2d 37 (D.C. Cir. 1985)

This was a unique case of federal government involvement in the operation of a local shelter, because the Washington, D.C.-based Community for Creative Non-Violence (CCNV) was using a previously vacant, federally owned building near the U.S. Capitol as an emergency shelter. Following a number of threatened closures and several highly publicized political actions, President Reagan had publicly promised to renovate the facility into a model shelter using federal funds. When the federal government backed out of the promise, CCNV and several homeless residents sued the administration, citing the president's pledge and other grounds. Although the court upheld the government's decision to close the building, the situation was reversed through public pressure and the building was renovated.

Burton v. New Jersey Department of Institutions and Agencies,
147 N.J. Super. Ct. 124 (1977)

A family of eight who had lost all their funds and their food stamp authorization card was denied emergency assistance because they continued to have a place to live, even though they had no resources to obtain food. The court interpreted the regulation in question to mean that homelessness and the provision of emergency assistance extend to those who require food and clothing as well as to those who require shelter.

Ross v. Board of Supervisors of Los Angeles County
(Cal. Ct. App. filed June 11, 1984)

This case built on the claims established in *Eisenheim*, asserting that, once the county had to provide emergency relief for those in need and without identification, officials could not provide nightly $8 checks to be used in hotels. The case claimed hotels were not available at this rate and that this rendered the aid meaningless.

7

Directory of
Organizations

Private Organizations and Associations

ACORN
522 Eighth Street, SE
Washington, DC 20003
(202) 547-9292
Mildred Brown, President

ACORN is a national organization of more than 75,000 grassroots low-
and moderate-income people seeking to change basic conditions of
poverty through local actions to turn over vacant housing to low-income
residents. Forty cities and 29 states have ACORN affiliates working on
issues of housing preservation and community development.

American Institute of Architects (AIA) Search for Shelter Program
1735 New York Avenue, NW
Washington, DC 20006
(202) 626-7468
Paul T. Knapp, Program Director

The Search for Shelter is an AIA program to assist local groups in meeting
the needs of homeless people. The program seeks to support the
development of local coalitions of providers, professionals, government
officials, and others to foster education and action in the community.

PUBLICATIONS: *The Search for Shelter,* articles from the 1986 symposia; *Search for Shelter* program workbook; *Creation of Shelter,* a follow-up volume, as well as related resources, such as an exhibit.

American Orthopsychiatric Association (ORTHO)
19 West Forty-fourth Street
New York, NY 10036
(212) 354-5770
Dr. Faith Parker, Associate Director

ORTHO focuses on preventive education of mental health professionals and community leaders in an effort to combine research, treatment, and social policy concerns. It has a Study Group on the homeless.

PUBLICATIONS: *American Journal of Orthopsychiatry* (quarterly); *Readings* (quarterly); and a newsletter.

American Planning Association
1776 Massachusetts Avenue, NW, Suite 704
Washington, DC 20036
(202) 872-0611
Israel Stollman, Executive Director

This professional organization provides research, information, and technical assistance on the full range of planning issues and policies at every level of government. Local chapters also develop educational programs.

PUBLICATIONS: *Journal of the American Planning Association* (quarterly); *Planning* (monthly); and other unrelated publications.

American Psychiatric Association
1400 K Street, NW
Washington, DC 20005
(202) 682-6000
Melvin Sabshin, M.D., Medical Director

The association is a professional and educational organization for those in the psychiatric field, especially those providing services to the homeless.

PUBLICATIONS: *American Journal of Psychiatry* (monthly); *Hospital and Community Psychiatry* (monthly); and a newsletter.

American Red Cross
National Headquarters
17th and D Streets, NW
Washington, DC 20006
(202) 639-3610
Enso V. Bighinatti, Contact Person

The Red Cross has traditionally provided services to those made homeless by disasters, such as fires or floods. More than 500 local chapters now provide services to the homeless through McKinney Act funding.

Bread for the World
802 Rhode Island Avenue, NE
Washington, DC 20018
(202) 269-0020
Art Simon, Director

This Christian citizens' movement treats hunger as a public policy issue; members are organized by congressional district to increase the effectiveness of their lobbying efforts. Study guides, organizing manuals, and other information on hunger is available.

Campus Outreach Opportunity League (COOL)
386 McNeal Hall, University of Minnesota
St. Paul, MN 55108
(612) 624-3018
Julia Scatliff, Executive Director

This national student organization promotes campus involvement in community action. COOL offers technical assistance to campus groups and hosts local and national conferences.

PUBLICATIONS: *Building a Movement: A Resource Book for Students in Community Service*; *On Your Mark, Go! Get Set*, a guide for starting a campus community service organization.

Cartoonists' Homeless Project c/o Senator David Roberti
107 South Broadway, Suite 3040
Los Angeles, CA 90012
(213) 620-3000
Chuck Elsesser, Contact Person

Participating artists dedicate panels on both the editorial and comic pages to the subject of homelessness in America.

Catholic Charities USA
1319 F Street, NW
Washington, DC 20004
(202) 639-8400
Fr. Thomas Harvey, Executive Director

This nationwide federation of organizations and individuals, including more than 600 agencies, is a traditional service provider to the hungry and homeless.

Center for Community Change
1000 Wisconsin Avenue, NW
Washington, DC 20007
(202) 342-0519
Pablo Eisenberg, President

Local community-based organizations can seek technical assistance in the areas of organizational development, funding, housing, and economic development.

PUBLICATIONS: "Community Change" (quarterly newsletter); *Housing Trust Funds,* by Mary Brooks, a guide to state programs for housing funds.

Center on Budget and Policy Priorities
236 Massachusetts Avenue, NE, Suite 305
Washington, DC 20002
(202) 544-0591
Robert Greenstein, Director

The center issues regular reports analyzing data and policy issues affecting poor Americans, including an annual report covering census data; reports on poverty among women, minorities, and rural residents; and analysis of federal budget issues and programs for the poor.

PUBLICATIONS: *Holes in the Safety Net: Poverty Programs and Policies in the States,* a national overview and 50 state reports; *A Place to Call Home,* a study of the housing crisis and the poor.

Child Welfare League of America (CWLA)
440 First Street, NW, Suite 310
Washington, DC 20001
(202) 638-2952
David Lieberman, Executive Director

CWLA is a membership organization of children's advocacy agencies, as well as public and voluntary organizations. It is active in the areas of research, training, and legislative advocacy on children's issues, including the needs of homeless children.

PUBLICATIONS: *Child Welfare* (bimonthly journal); *Washington Social Legislation Bulletin* (biweekly report); "Homeless Children and Families."

Children's Defense Fund (CDF)
122 C Street, NW
Washington, DC 20001
(202) 628-8787
Marian Wright Edelman, President

CDF's goal is to educate policymakers about the needs of poor and minority children. It monitors federal and state policy and legislation on health, education, child welfare, mental health, teen pregnancy, and youth employment.

PUBLICATIONS: *CDF Reports,* monthly update on relevant issues; *A Children's Defense Budget,* annual exhaustive analysis of federal budget proposals and their effects on children; other specialized reports and fact books are also published.

Coalition on Human Needs
1000 Wisconsin Avenue, NW
Washington, DC 20007
(202) 342-0726
Susan Rees, Executive Director

A wide range of groups concerned with issues affecting low-income people participate in this coalition, which seeks to reduce poverty and improve the education and welfare systems. Research assistance and legislative information are provided to affiliates.

PUBLICATIONS: *The National Technical Assistance Directory: A Guide for State Advocates and Service Providers,* a directory of national organizations that provide technical assistance and analytical publications.

Comic Relief
2049 Century Park East, Suite 4250
Los Angeles, CA 90067
(213) 201-9317
Bob Zmuda, President

This annual marathon comedy performance benefit was first broadcast in 1986, raising $2.5 million. The 1989 show, featuring dozens of nationally known comedians, raised well over $4 million for homeless health care programs around the country.

Community for Creative Non-Violence (CCNV)
425 Second Street, NW
Washington, DC 20001
(202) 393-1909
Mitch Snyder, Spokesperson

CCNV is a direct service and public advocacy organization that provides information on homelessness at a national level and offers nationwide referrals to volunteer opportunities through the National Volunteer Clearinghouse on the Homeless (800-HELP-664).

PUBLICATION: *Homelessness in America: A Forced March to Nowhere.*

Council of Large Public Housing Authorities (CLPHA)
7 Marshall Street
Boston, MA 02108
(617) 742-3720
Robert E. McKay, Executive Director

Public housing authority directors who manage more than 1,200 units constitute the membership of this organization, which provides information and updates on federal legislation and policy matters affecting managers and residents of the nation's public housing developments.

PUBLICATIONS: *Public Housing Today* and *Public Housing Tomorrow* profile the residents, costs, problems, and needs of public housing.

Council of State Community Affairs Agencies (COSCAA)
Hall of States
444 North Capitol Street, NE, Suite 251
Washington, DC 20001
(202) 393-6435
John M. Sidor, Executive Director

This national network of state-level community affairs officials working on homeless programs monitors federal legislation on homelessness and housing, as well as state initiatives for affordable housing.

PUBLICATION: "States and Housing," a newsletter.

Council of State Governments
Iron Works Pike, P.O. Box 11910
Lexington, KY 40578
(606) 252-2291
Carl Stenberg, Executive Director

A joint agency of all state governments, this organization researches topics ranging from state housing programs to welfare policy. It acts as an information service for agencies, officials, and legislators and promotes cooperation and liaison between all levels of government.

Covenant House
440 Ninth Avenue
New York, NY 10001
(202) 613-0300

Covenant House offers shelter and services for homeless teenagers in a dozen locations in North and Central America. It also operates a national "Nineline" (1-800-999-9999) for runaways and their parents to seek help.

Enterprise Foundation
American City Building, Suite 505
Columbia, MD 21044
(301) 964-1230
James Rouse, President

More than 100 nonprofit and neighborhood groups belong to this network, which seeks ways to move people out of poverty and into self-sufficiency and decent housing.

PUBLICATION: "Network News," a newsletter.

Food Research and Action Center (FRAC)
1319 F Street, NW, Suite 500
Washington, DC 20004
(202) 393-5060
Robert Fersh, Director

FRAC's primary strategy is to reduce hunger in the United States through the improvement of federal food programs. It acts as a clearinghouse on public policy, legislation, technical assistance, education, and the formation of statewide coalitions on the issue.

PUBLICATIONS: "Foodlines" (monthly newsletter); *FRAC's Guide to the Food Stamp Program*; *WIC Facts.*

Homelessness Information Exchange
1830 Connecticut Avenue, NW, 4th Floor
Washington, DC 20009
(202) 462-7551
Dana Harris, Director

This education and information service performs custom research on questions related to homelessness, as well as providing other resources including a computerized bibliography and a forthcoming database of model programs.

PUBLICATIONS: "Homewords" (quarterly newsletter); assorted information packets.

Housing Assistance Council (HAC)
1025 Vermont Avenue, NW, Suite 606
Washington, DC 20005
(202) 842-8600
Harold Wilson, Executive Director

HAC provides technical assistance, loans, research, and information on rural low-income housing development, especially Farmers Home Administration programs. It publishes regular reports on federal rural programs and trends in rural poverty and development.

PUBLICATIONS: "HAC News" (biweekly newsletter); "State Action Memorandum" (bimonthly newsletter); *HAC Technical Manuals* on rural housing and community issues.

Housing Trust Fund Project
570 Shepard Street
San Pedro, CA 90731
(213) 833-4249
Mary Brooks, Director

Neighborhood groups can receive technical assistance from this project, which monitors the 41 housing trust funds in the various states.

PUBLICATION: "News from the Housing Trust Fund Project," a newsletter.

Institute for Community Economics (ICE)
151 Montague City Road
Greenfield, MA 01301
(413) 774-7956
Chuck Matthei, Executive Director

ICE provides technical and financial assistance to housing and economic development projects in low-income communities via a community loan fund; it offers educational resources and services to a wide range of constituencies. Its efforts are based on the community land trust model, and its revolving loan fund has supported programs in 22 states.

PUBLICATIONS: *The Community Land Trust Handbook*; *Community Loan Fund Manual*; *Directory of Socially Responsible Investments*; "Community Economics" (newsletter).

Institute for Policy Studies (IPS)
1601 Connecticut Avenue, NW
Washington, DC 20009
(202) 234-9382
Chester Hartman, Domestic Security Project

IPS is a research and education center that recently produced "A Progressive Housing Policy for America," the foundations for pending major federal housing legislation.

Jobs with Peace Campaign
76 Summer Street
Boston, MA 02110
(617) 338-5738
Michael Brown, Director

Grassroots organizing and action to redirect federal spending priorities to affordable housing and other human needs is the focus of this organization, which has chapters in ten cities. The organization has a national campaign underway entitled "Build Homes not Bombs." Technical assistance is provided in developing an organization, identifying local issues, and fundraising, as well as handling local media.

PUBLICATION: Build Homes not Bombs organizing kit.

Local Initiatives Support Corporation (LISC)
666 Third Avenue
New York, NY 10017
(212) 949-8560
Paul Grogan, Director

This project of the Ford Foundation offers financing and technical assistance to nonprofit organizations working on community development and low-income housing by channeling private sector resources into more than 120 cities.

Mental Health Law Project (MHLP)
2021 L Street, NW
Washington, DC 20036
(202) 467-5730
Norman Rosenberg, Director

MHLP is a legal advocacy organization for the rights of the mentally disabled and it is active in public education and information.

PUBLICATION: *Update,* published six times a year.

National Alliance for the Mentally Ill (NAMI)
1901 North Fort Myer Drive, Suite 500
Arlington, VA 22209
(703) 524-7600
Laurie Flynn, National Executive Director

This national advocacy and research organization for the mentally ill seeks to create a coordinated system of care.

PUBLICATION: "The NAMI Advocate," a bimonthly newsletter.

National Alliance To End Homelessness
1518 K Street, NW, Suite 206
Washington, DC 20005
(202) 638-1526
Thomas L. Kenyon, Executive Director

The alliance is a coalition of corporations, service providers, and individuals that uses research and public education in its efforts to address homelessness.

PUBLICATION: *Housing and Homelessness,* a special report.

National Association of Community Health Centers (NACHC)
1330 New Hampshire Avenue, NW, Suite 122
Washington, DC 20036
(202) 659-8008
Freda Mitchem, Homeless Health Care Coordinator

This membership organization represents McKinney-funded Health Care for the Homeless projects, as well as other health care providers and migrant health centers. NACHC provides technical assistance, training, and public policy information.

PUBLICATIONS: *Streetreach* (quarterly); a national directory of Homeless Health Care Projects.

National Association of Housing and Redevelopment Officials (NAHRO)
1320 Eighteenth Street, NW, 5th Floor
Washington, DC 20036
(202) 429-2960
Richard Y. Nelson, Executive Director

NAHRO offers information services and policy presentations to housing officials at all levels of government.

National Association of Social Workers (NASW)
7981 Eastern Avenue
Silver Spring, MD 20910
(301) 565-0333
Mark Battle, Executive Director

NASW conducts the "There's No Place Like Home" campaign of public education on homelessness. The organization makes available informative material on homelessness and reasons people should become involved to alleviate the problem.

National Clearinghouse for Legal Services
407 South Dearborn, Suite 400
Chicago, IL 60609
(312) 939-3830
Michael Leonard, Executive Director

The clearinghouse accesses documents related to legal issues and provides them for general distribution.

PUBLICATION: *Homelessness in America: A Litigation Memorandum for Legal Services Advocates.*

National Coalition for the Homeless
105 East Twenty-second Street
New York, NY 10010
(212) 460-8110
Mary Ellen Hombs, Director

This federation of service providers and advocates acts as a national network for enacting and monitoring legislation and litigation related to the homeless.

PUBLICATIONS: "Safety Network" (monthly newsletter); numerous reports on local and national aspects of homelessness and related issues; model legislation and programs.

National Conference of State Legislatures (NCSL)
1050 Seventeenth Street, Suite 2100
Denver, CO 80265
(303) 623-7800
William T. Pound, Executive Director

NCSL serves the members of the nation's 50 state legislatures, through publications and other tools, with current information on state and federal public policy issues.

PUBLICATIONS: *State Legislatures* (ten times annually); "Federal Update" (newsletter); *State Legislative Report,* a policy update; *Directory of Legislative Leaders,* a national guide.

National Council of Community Health Centers
12300 Twinbrook Parkway, Suite 320
Rockville, MD 20852
(301) 984-6200
Charles Ray, Executive Director

This trade association of mental health service providers seeks to affect public policy and service delivery to those in need of mental health care.

National Council of La Raza
810 First Street, NE, Suite 500
Washington, DC 20002
(202) 289-1551
Raul Yzaguirre, President

An improved quality of life for Hispanic Americans is the purpose of this umbrella organization, which has affiliations with more than 4,000 Hispanic groups nationwide. The organization provides technical assistance, public education materials, public policy analysis, and advocacy on behalf of its constituency.

PUBLICATION: "The Hispanic Housing Crisis," a newsletter.

National Governors' Association (NGA)
Hall of States
444 North Capitol Street, NE
Washington, DC 20001
(202) 624-5300
Raymond Scheppach, Executive Director

NGA monitors the McKinney Act and related legislation for the state governors and produces information on model programs.

PUBLICATION: "Status of Programs under the Stewart B. McKinney Homeless Assistance Act and Related Legislation."

National Housing Institute (NHI)
439 Main Street
Orange, NJ 07050
(201) 678-3110
David Steinglass, Director

NHI is an education and research organization focused on low-income housing.

PUBLICATION: *Shelterforce* magazine, published six times a year.

National Housing Law Project (NHLP)
1950 Addison Street
Berkeley, CA 94704
(415) 548-9400
Frances Werner, Director

NHLP is a back-up center to advise and assist local Legal Services lawyers working on housing and community development issues, including shelter and homelessness problems.

PUBLICATIONS: *Housing Law Bulletin* (bimonthly); numerous manuals on federal housing programs.

National League of Cities (NLC)
1301 Pennsylvania Avenue, NW
Washington, DC 20004
(202) 626-3030
Alan Beals, Executive Director

NLC seeks to develop a national policy that addresses the needs of urban Americans. It provides information, technical assistance, and training to local officials on the federal tools available to alleviate pressing urban problems.

PUBLICATIONS: *Children, Families & Cities: Programs that Work at the Local Level; Poverty in America: New Data, New Perspectives.*

National Low Income Housing Coalition (NLIHC)
Low Income Housing Information Service (LIHIS)
1012 Fourteenth Street, NW
Washington, DC 20005
(202) 662-1530
Barry Zigas, President

NLIHC is focused on education, advocacy, and organizing for low-income housing. LIHIS emphasizes federal housing programs and policies.

PUBLICATIONS: *Low Income Housing Round-Up* (monthly); *Special Memorandum,* supplements on specific housing topics.

National Mental Health Association (NMHA)
1021 Prince Street
Alexandria, VA 22314
(202) 684-7722
Preston Garrison, Director

NMHA works to improve mental health services, prevent mental illness, and promote mental health through citizen effort. It has 600 local and state affiliated groups across the country.

PUBLICATIONS: *For Homeless People with Mental Illness: Action Guidelines*; *The Role of Community Foundations in Meeting the Needs of Homeless Individuals with Mental Illnesses*; "FOCUS" (newsletter); *Homeless in America* (video).

National Network of Runaway Youth Services
1400 I Street, NW, Suite 330
Washington, DC 20005
(202) 682-4114
June Bucy, Executive Director

More than 1,000 local shelter programs are members of this network, which sponsors training, offers information, and sponsors a national telecommunications system for youth programs.

National Resource Center on Homelessness and Mental Illness
Policy Research Associates
262 Delaware Avenue
Delmar, NY 12054
800-444-7415
Deborah Dennis, Project Director

This center, under contract to the federal government, provides technical assistance and other information on services needed by homeless mentally ill people. It maintains a database of published and unpublished work and offers bibliographies, custom searches, and other material.

PUBLICATIONS: *Access* (quarterly); a national organizational referral list of groups working in the field of homelessness.

National Shared Housing Resource Center
6344 Greene Street
Philadelphia, PA 19144
(215) 848-1220
Joyce Mantel, Director

Shared housing is being sought by more and more people as housing costs rise. This organization offers information, technical assistance, resource development, and training to individuals, community organizations, and public agencies.

National Student Campaign against Hunger (NSCAH)
29 Temple Place
Boston, MA 02111
(617) 292-4823
Leslie Samuelrich, Campaign Director

NSCAH combines the efforts of 20 state Public Interest Research Groups (PIRGs) and USA for Africa to aid students in fighting hunger. A major campus event is promoted each semester, and NSCAH provides technical assistance and acts as a clearinghouse for projects.

PUBLICATION: "Students Making a Difference," a newsletter.

National Union of the Homeless
2001 Spring Garden Street
Philadelphia, PA 19130
(215) 972-7085
Leona Smith, President

The union is the only national self-help effort of homeless people, with membership chapters in numerous cities. The union focuses on leadership training and political activity by those in shelters or on the streets in the areas of housing, jobs, education, and health.

Robert Wood Johnson Foundation
Program on Chronic Mental Illness
74 Fenwood Road
Boston, MA 02115
(617) 738-7774
Dr. Miles Shore, Director

The Johnson Foundation is funding a five-year demonstration program on chronic mental illness in nine of the nation's largest cities, similar to its Health Care for the Homeless program, initiated in the early 1980s.

PUBLICATION: *Housing for People with Mental Illness: A Guide for Development.*

Salvation Army
National Public Affairs Office
1025 Vermont Avenue, NW
Washington, DC 20005
(202) 639-8414
Colonel Ernest A. Miller, Director

This international religious charity is one of the historic providers of shelter and alcohol rehabilitation services, with more than 10,000 local chapters.

Second Harvest
343 South Dearborn, Suite 410
Chicago, IL 60604
(312) 341-1303
Steven Whitehead, Executive Director

PRIVATE ORGANIZATIONS AND ASSOCIATIONS   111

This food-banking network is the largest nongovernment food program in the nation, intercepting tons of surplus edible food and routing it to 38,000 charitable organizations for use in local relief efforts.

Share Our Strength (S.O.S.)
1511 K Street, NW, Suite 632
Washington, DC 20005
(202) 393-2925
Bill Shore, Executive Director

This nationwide organization of over 2,000 restaurateurs, chefs, and other food service professionals conducts a "Fight Food Waste" campaign to provide information to donors who might want to offer surplus food to the needy. S.O.S. also promotes an annual national event to raise funds for local hunger relief.

United States Conference of Mayors
1620 I Street, NW
Washington, DC 20005
(202) 293-7330
J. Thomas Cochran, Executive Director

The Conference of Mayors is an education and lobbying organization for mayors, providing background information and position statements on vital issues. Its Task Force on Hunger and Homelessness conducts an annual survey of member cities and their services and conditions.

PUBLICATION: *The Continued Growth of Hunger, Homelessness, and Poverty in America's Cities,* an annual report.

United Way of America
701 North Fairfax Street
Alexandria, VA 22314
(703) 836-7100
William I. Fields, Director

United Way helps fund and coordinate many local and national programs for the homeless and hungry.

Voices from the Streets
3344 Prospect Street, NW
Washington, DC 20007
(202) 333-8671
Suzanne Goldman, Director

Voices from the Streets was organized in 1987 to present a play of the same name to the members of Congress on the eve of their vote on the Stewart B. McKinney Homeless Assistance Act. The ensemble of "Voices" actors— homeless adults and children and their advocates—tell the stories of who they are, how they got there, and what their possibilities are. Voices is also an organization devoted to developing an arts curriculum, including African dance, cartooning, oil painting, drama, Shakespeare, creative writing, gospel choir, and pantomime, in Washington shelters for the homeless.

Volunteers of America (VOA)
3813 North Causeway Boulevard
Metairie, LA 70002
(504) 837-2652
Raymond Tremont, President

VOA operates more than 400 local programs for the homeless, the elderly, alcoholics, and drug users.

Women's Institute for Housing and Economic Development
179 South Street
Boston, MA 02111
(617) 423-2296
Marcie Laden, Executive Director

This nonprofit group offers technical assistance to social service agencies and community-based women's organizations seeking to develop emergency shelter, transitional housing, and permanent housing for low-income women.

PUBLICATIONS: *A Development Primer: Starting Housing and Business Ventures by and/or for Women; A Manual on Transitional Housing.*

Federal Agencies

Federal Emergency Management Agency (FEMA)
National Emergency Food and Shelter Board
601 North Fairfax Street, Suite 225
Alexandria, VA 22314
(703) 683-1166
Robert G. Chappell, Chair

The FEMA board administers emergency McKinney Act funds for nonprofit organizations serving the homeless with food, shelter, transportation, emergency rent or mortgage assistance, or first month's rent. Membership of the national board, which makes grants to local boards, is composed of United Way of America, American Red Cross, Catholic Charities, Council of Jewish Federations, Salvation Army, and the Council of Churches.

General Services Administration (GSA)
General Services Building
Washington, DC 20405
(202) 525-0800
Richard Austin, Acting Director

GSA is responsible for McKinney Act provisions to make underutilized federal space and buildings available to assist the homeless. The agency also administers a similar requirement affecting state surplus personal property.

Health Resources and Services Administration (HRSA)
5600 Fishers Lane
Rockville, MD 20857
(301) 443-8134
David N. Sundwall, M.D., Administrator

HRSA is an agency of HHS mandated by the McKinney Act to administer primary health care, drug and alcohol abuse treatment, and mental health services for the homeless.

Interagency Council on the Homeless
451 Seventh Street, SW, Room 10158
Washington, DC 20410
(202) 755-1480
Patricia Carlile, Executive Director

The council fulfills a McKinney Act requirement that HUD convene a working group of all participating agencies to review, monitor, evaluate, and recommend improvements to the McKinney Act. The council is also mandated to provide technical assistance and publish a regular newsletter, "Council Communiqué."

National Institute of Mental Health (NIMH)
Office of Programs for the Homeless Mentally Ill
5600 Fishers Lane
Rockville, MD 20857
(301) 443-3706
Louis Judd, M.D., Director

NIMH, a component of HHS, oversees the block grant provisions of the McKinney Act for community-based mental health services, funded through the states and operated by private and nonprofit providers. It also operates the McKinney-funded program for state mental health authorities to establish community pilot programs for homeless adults and children with severe long-term mental illnesses.

National Institute on Alcohol Abuse and Alcoholism (NIAAA)
5600 Fishers Lane
Rockville, MD 20857
(301) 443-0786
Enoch Gordis, M.D., Director

The NIAAA, a component of HHS, administers the McKinney Act alcohol and drug abuse demonstration grant program and disseminates information on program models.

U.S. Bureau of the Census
Suitland, MD 20233
(301) 763-5190
John G. Keane, Director

The agency conducts a count of homeless people in conjunction with the national count each decade. Its efforts in 1980 were criticized by shelter providers and advocates as unrealistic and ineffective; it undertook a partial count of the homeless in 1990.

U.S. Department of Agriculture (USDA)
Fourteenth Street and Independence Avenue, NW
Washington, DC 20250
(202) 447-3631
Clayton K. Yeutter, Secretary

USDA, through the Food and Nutrition Service, administers the Food Stamp and McKinney Act regulations to aid homeless people. In addition, it manages the Temporary Emergency Food Assistance Program (TEFAP) to provide surplus food commodities to the homeless. The Farmers Home Administration (FmHA), an agency of USDA, operates two programs to make foreclosed Section 502 rural homes available to the homeless.

U.S. Department of Education
400 Maryland Avenue, SW
Washington, DC 20202
(202) 732-3000
Lauro F. Cavazos, Secretary

The agency oversees a McKinney Act program to fund state plans for ensuring that homeless children have free, appropriate educational services and are not denied access to schools because they lack a permanent address. The agency also makes grants to state education agencies to develop adult literacy programs for homeless people.

U.S. Department of Health and Human Services (HHS)
200 Independence Avenue, SW
Washington, DC 20201
(202) 245-6296
Louis W. Sullivan, Secretary

HHS oversees the McKinney Act program to provide primary health care to homeless people through public and private nonprofit organizations. Component parts of the agency also administer other portions of the legislation; these are listed separately in this section.

U.S. Department of Housing and Urban Development (HUD)
451 Seventh Street, SW
Washington, DC 20410
(202) 655-4000
Jack F. Kemp, Secretary

HUD administers a variety of low-income housing programs, with components involving housing for homeless people. These include conventional public housing projects as well as other forms of assisted and subsidized housing. HUD also operates the Emergency Shelter Grant Program (ESGP) under the McKinney Act, with block grants to fund (1) expansion of existing shelters and conversion of new buildings, and (2) the provision of services for shelter residents. The McKinney Act also funds transitional housing for deinstitutionalized and mentally disabled individuals and families with children, as well as permanent housing for the handicapped.

U.S. Department of Labor
200 Constitution Avenue, NW
Washington, DC 20210
(202) 523-0682
Elizabeth H. Dole, Secretary

Under the McKinney Act, the agency administers a job training demonstration program for homeless people, as well as an employment program to reintegrate homeless veterans.

U.S. Department of Veterans Affairs (VA)
810 Vermont Avenue, NW
Washington, DC 20420
(202) 233-2300
Edward J. Derwinski, Administrator of Veterans Affairs

The VA operates the McKinney Act domiciliary care program to use surplus space in VA hospitals as shelter beds for homeless veterans. The agency also administers a 1987 program to make single-family homes foreclosed from VA loans available for homeless veterans and their families.

8

Reference Materials

Activism and Advocacy

Day, Dorothy. **The Long Loneliness: An Autobiography.** New York: Harper and Row, 1981. 286p. $5.95. ISBN 0-06-061751-9.

In the decades preceding the 1980s, there were two significant sources of help for the homeless: the traditional missions and Salvation Army establishments, and the Catholic Worker (CW) Houses of Hospitality spread around the nation. This book, by the cofounder of the CW movement and its newspaper editor for over 30 years, tells of the Depression-era founding of the small shelters and soup lines that still exist today, as well as the story of Day's longtime leadership on issues of social justice, peace, and racial equality.

Miller, William. **Dorothy Day: A Biography.** New York: Harper and Row, 1982. 527p. $10.95. ISBN 0-06-065752-8.

This biography of Catholic Worker cofounder Dorothy Day offers a candid portrait of her work in the social justice movement.

National Coalition for the Homeless. **Doing Good Well: A Report on Hands Across America Funding.** New York: National Coalition for the Homeless (105 East Twenty-second Street, New York, NY 10010), 1986. 35p. $4.

The one-day event of Americans linking hands across the nation to raise funds for the fight against hunger and homelessness spurred the growth of many activities. This report examines how those funds were distributed and used.

————. **Making a Difference: A Resource Guide on Homelessness for Students.** New York: National Coalition for the Homeless (105 East Twenty-second Street, New York, NY 10010), 1989. 82p. $8

Many students have become active in their college communities, volunteering to help the hungry and homeless. Some of those already involved tell their stories here, with suggestions on how to start a local project and how to locate national organizations and educational resources.

Rader, Victoria. **Signal through the Flames: Mitch Snyder and America's Homeless.** Kansas City, MO: Sheed & Ward, 1986. 272p. $10.95. ISBN 0-934134-24-3.

The work of Washington, D.C.'s Community for Creative Non-Violence is explored here from a campaign viewpoint, with the development of the organization's various public efforts for peace and justice explored from inception to retrospective analysis. Significant insight into the workings of the community result from the availability of community members past and present, as well as the use of the group's extensive archives on its work.

Ward, Jim. **Organizing for the Homeless.** Ottawa: Canadian Council on Social Development, 1989. 117p. $15. ISBN 0-88810-390-5.

While homeless people themselves have taken steps to organize on their own behalf, very few written works address the need for this action or the issues involved when non-homeless people try to foster such empowerment among the homeless. The importance and particulars of organizing are stressed here, along with insights into supporting homeless-driven efforts to address larger institutions and to raise funds.

AIDS

The Partnership for the Homeless. **AIDS—The Cutting Edge of Homelessness in New York City.** New York: The Partnership for the Homeless, 1989. 48p.

The partnership operates an extensive network of voluntary shelters in churches and synagogues in New York City. Here it examines the impact and future influence of AIDS on the homeless population of that city, proposing its own plan for housing-care assistance.

Report of the Presidential Commission on the Human Immunodeficiency Virus Epidemic. Washington, DC: U.S. Government Printing Office, June 1988. 201p. $11. GPO 0-214-701: QL 3.

This report examines a number of aspects of the HIV epidemic, with a chapter devoted to the disproportionate impact of HIV on the poor. Drug abuse and treatment are discussed, with a recommendation that treatment on demand be a goal. The special needs of the homeless person who is HIV-seropositive are also examined.

Shilts, Randy. **And the Band Played On: Politics, People and the AIDS Epidemic.** New York: St. Martin's, 1987. 613p. $12.95. ISBN 0-14-011-369-x.

Widely heralded as the definitive documentary study of how AIDS developed into a major health and social issue in the United States, this book traces the beginning of the infection from pre-1980 identification as a gay disease to the mid-1980s, when it became a political and social issue as well as a health problem.

U.S. General Accounting Office. **AIDS Education: Issues Affecting Counseling and Testing Programs.** Washington, DC: U.S. General Accounting Office, February 1989. 15p. GAO/HRD-89-39.

With neither a vaccine nor a cure available for AIDS, education is considered mandatory to control the spread of the epidemic. Testing, follow-up and long-term counseling, partner notification, outreach to intravenous drug users, and antidiscrimination protections are examined here for their effect on the need for and use of education about AIDS. For instance, investigation revealed that, while 34 percent of AIDS cases nationwide involve IV drug use, none of the health departments studied for this report had undertaken any outreach to drug users.

————. **AIDS Forecasting: Undercount of Cases and Lack of Key Data Weaken Existing Estimates.** Washington, DC: U.S. General Accounting Office, June 1989. 102p. GAO/PEMD-89-13. An assessment of national forecasts of the future of the AIDS epidemic, this report offers a detailed explanation of the major models for predicting the spread of the fatal disease. An extensive bibliography of studies is provided.

Alcoholism

National Institute on Alcohol Abuse and Alcoholism (NIAAA). **Alcohol Health & Research World: Homelessness,** vol. 2, no. 3 (Spring 1987). 92p. DHHS Publication No. (ADM) 87-151.

This special edition of NIAAA's monthly journal contains 20 articles and features on medical and nonmedical aspects of alcohol and the homeless. Long one of the most stereotyped problems of the homeless, alcohol dependence is increasingly being treated as a serious health problem that also requires housing as a solution.

————. **Alcohol Recovery Programs for Homeless People: A Survey of Current Programs in the U.S.** Washington, DC: U.S. Government Printing Office, 1988. 125p. GPO 201-875-83661.

The homeless alcoholic is one of the most enduring stereotypes of the unsheltered person. This survey of programs nominated by those who work with the homeless and with alcoholics examines intake programs, primary and sustained recovery settings, comprehensive services, and alcohol-free housing models that are targeted to indigent alcoholics.

Children and Families

Bach, Victor, and Renee Steinhagen. **Alternatives to the Welfare Hotel: Using Emergency Assistance to Provide Decent Transitional Shelter for Homeless Families.** New York: Community Service Society (105 East Twenty-second Street, New York, NY 10010), 1987. 56p. $6.50.

Family homelessness in New York City is examined, as well as alternative models for shelter operated with emergency assistance funds. This report advances the idea that short-term shelters can become permanent low-income housing.

Born, Catherine E. **Our Future and Our Only Hope: A Survey of City Halls Regarding Children and Families.** Washington, DC: National League of Cities (NLC), September 1989. 118p. $15. ISBN 0-933729-52-9.

The NLC surveyed city halls around the nation to find the most pressing issues for children and families. Families ranked the shortage of affordable housing highest in the list of priorities. A wide variety of successful local programs, in areas ranging from housing to substance abuse to family support, are profiled.

Children's Defense Fund. **A Vision for America's Future: An Agenda for the 1990's—A Children's Defense Budget.** Washington, DC: Children's Defense Fund, 1989. 150p. $11.95. ISBN 0-938008-67-6.

This annual profile of issues affecting children offers analytical and anecdotal information on health, family income, housing, homelessness, food assistance, children at risk, child care, and young families; factual material on poverty, infant mortality, public expenditures on children, voting records of officials on children's issues; and comparative figures on children in the cities, states, nation, and world.

The Johns Hopkins University Institute for Policy Studies. **Homeless Children and Youth: Coping with a National Tragedy.** Papers presented at a national conference on April 25–28, 1989, Washington, D.C. Baltimore, MD: Johns Hopkins University Press, 1989. $30.

This conference assembled many of the leading researchers, advocates, policymakers, and foundation and corporate leaders in the field of child and family homelessness. The 12 commissioned papers included in the resulting report assess the causes and size of the problem and possible solutions. A dozen working models of service delivery are examined, and an agenda for local, state, and federal action is presented.

Kozol, Jonathan. **Rachel and Her Children: Homeless Families in America.** New York: Ballantine Books, 1989. 261p. $8.95. ISBN 0-449-90339-7.

This vivid account of life in the welfare hotels of New York City demonstrates not only the financial waste of this method for serving homeless families, but also the damage done to young lives and struggling parents. Alongside the personal stories told by mothers, fathers, and children are the chilling statistics that explain how poverty works in daily life.

National Coalition for the Homeless. **Broken Lives: Denial of Education to Homeless Children.** New York: National Coalition for the Homeless (105 East Twenty-second Street, New York, NY 10010), December 1987. $5. 32p.

A detailed analysis of the obstacles to education faced by homeless children, even after the passage of the McKinney Act requirements for access to education.

National League of Cities. **Children, Families & Cities: Programs that Work at the Local Level.** Washington, DC: National League of Cities, 1987. 201p. $15. ISBN 0-933729-32-4.

Program profiles of more than three dozen local efforts to address child and family issues, including homelessness, make up this directory, which provides project contacts and lessons learned.

U.S. Congress. House. Committee on Government Operations. **Homeless Families: A Neglected Crisis.** 99th Cong., 2d sess., 1986. H. Rept. 99-982. 24p.

This brief report, based on a congressional study, examines the causes of family homelessness, finds that the use of the Emergency Assistance program shelter system is harmful for homeless families, and makes recommendations for change.

U.S. General Accounting Office. **Children and Youths: About 68,000 Homeless and 186,000 in Shared Housing at Any Given Time.** Washington, DC: U.S. General Accounting Office, June 1989. 40p. GAO/PEMD-89-14.

One of several studies mandated by the McKinney Act, this report seeks to estimate the number of children and youth who are homeless. The study not only attempts to quantify those who are in shelters or on the streets, but also accepts the McKinney homeless definition to mean that those who are "precariously housed" include those living in doubled-up housing arrangements with friends or relatives.

————. **Pediatric AIDS: Health and Social Service Needs of Infants and Children.** Washington, DC: U.S. General Accounting Office, May 1989. 20p. GAO/HRD-89-96.

With homelessness and drug use on the rise among the poor, pediatric AIDS, which operates medically in children in forms different than in adults, is also on the increase. Such children often have parents with a history of drug use, and these parents have a greater likelihood of having AIDS. AIDS is now the leading cause of death for children up to age four in New York City; homelessness is a likely accompaniment or consequence of AIDS infection.

Counting the Homeless

Community for Creative Non-Violence (CCNV). **A Forced March to Nowhere—Homelessness: A National Priority.** Washington, DC: Community for Creative Non-Violence (425 Second Street, NW, Washington, DC 20001), September 1980. 87p. $5.

In 1980, the U.S. House of Representatives Committee on the District of Columbia sought to compare the little-known problem of homelessness in the nation's capital to the difficulties faced in the rest of the nation. CCNV, a Washington-based service and advocacy organization, prepared this testimony after canvassing service providers and officials around the states.

Hombs, Mary Ellen, and Mitch Snyder. **Homelessness in America: A Forced March to Nowhere.** 2d ed. Washington, D.C.: Community for Creative Non-Violence (425 Second Street, NW, Washington, DC 20001), 1983. 146p. $5. ISBN 0-686-39879-3.

This national survey of homelessness and its origins was first released in conjunction with the original 1982 congressional hearings of the same title. When it was updated the following year, it included the estimates of national homelessness that engendered national controversy.

Horowitz, Carl F. **"Mitch Snyder's Phony Numbers: The Fiction of Three Million Homeless."** The Heritage Foundation *Policy Review* (Summer 1989): 66–69.

This article attempts to refute the estimates of homeless advocate Mitch Snyder, who has repeatedly stated that three million Americans are homeless. Certain portions of other research efforts are summarized in support of the author's argument.

Kondratas, S. Anna. **"Myth, Reality, and the Homeless."** *Insight* (April 14, 1986): 73.

The author, the chief public defender of government efforts at counting the homeless, became, in 1989, the HUD official in charge of homeless programs. Here, as a policy analyst for The Heritage Foundation, she addresses three assertions about the homeless: that there are very large numbers of them, that the Reagan administration worsened their condition by its policies, and that the federal government is failing to help them.

———. **"A Strategy for Helping America's Homeless."** The Heritage Foundation *Backgrounder*, No. 431 (May 6, 1985): 144–149.

The author argues against expanded federal involvement as the cure for increased homelessness, asserting that volunteer, state, and local efforts are needed to assist those in need.

Milburn, Norweeta G., Roderick J. Watts, and Susan L. Anderson. **An Analysis of Current Research Methods for Studying the Homeless.** Washington, DC: Institute for Urban Affairs and Research, Howard University, 1984. 44p.

An overview of research techniques of the last two decades is presented, with the goal of determining previous definitions of homelessness, subgroups studied, research methods, data collected, and gaps in content. The authors conclude that there have been serious deficiencies in previous work, making it of extremely limited use in policy development.

National Academy of Sciences, Institute of Medicine. **Homelessness, Health and Human Needs.** Washington, DC: National Academy Press, 1988. 165p. $19.95. ISBN 0-309-03832-4.

This controversial report had a congressional mandate to assess the provision of health care services to the homeless. The resulting work provides background data and recommendations on housing, income, employment, mental illness, and deinstitutionalization as these subjects relate to the problem. The document was debated on its release, when 10 of the 13 experts who contributed to it released a supplemental report calling for national action on housing, wages, and benefits to fight homelessness. This report is available from the United Hospital Fund Publications Program, 55 Fifth Avenue, New York, NY 10003.

Tucker, William. **"America's Homeless: Victims of Rent Control."** The Heritage Foundation *Backgrounder* No. 685 (January 12, 1989). 12p.

The size of the problem of homelessness is studied from the perspective of conservative political thought that sees the tight housing markets of some cities with large homeless populations as being directly connected to the presence of rent regulation. The author relies on the data of the 1984 HUD report for his claims.

U.S. Congress. House. Committee on Banking, Finance, and Urban Affairs and Committee on Government Operations. **Joint Hearing on the HUD Report on Homelessness.** 98th Cong. 2d sess., 1984. 418p.

The 1984 HUD report on homelessness was controversial both for the numerical conclusions it reached about the size of the problem and for the methodology used in reaching those conclusions. Though much was written and said about the report, this hearing presented a range of testimony from those involved, including interviewers, interviewees, and social scientists who assessed the results.

U.S. Department of Housing and Urban Development (HUD). **Publications Relating to Homelessness: A Working Bibliography.** Washington, DC: HUD Office of Policy Development and Research, 1989. 53p.

This comprehensive bibliography offers listings of state and local reports on homelessness, executive and legislative studies, reports from service providers and public interest groups, and categories of subject matter reports, such as studies of mental health, children, and nutrition.

————. **A Report on the 1988 National Survey of Shelters for the Homeless.** Washington, DC: HUD Office of Policy Development and Research, 1989. 55p.

This HUD report attempts to quantify the nature of assistance efforts being made for homeless people. Its brief survey of service providers found, among other things, that the number of shelters in the nation had tripled from 1984 to 1988 and that spending had increased fivefold.

————. **A Report to the Secretary on the Homeless and Emergency Shelter.** Washington, DC: HUD Office of Policy Development and Research, 1984. 67p.

This initial effort by the federal government to assess the problem of homelessness resulted in enormous controversy. Focus was on this report's methodology, which utilized an obscure commercial marketing measurement of population as the basis for interviewing local shelter providers about the size of the homeless population. The result was a national estimate of 250,000–350,000 homeless.

Urban Institute. **Feeding the Homeless: Does the Prepared Meals Provision Help? Report to Congress on the Prepared Meal Provision.** Washington, DC: Urban Institute Project Report, 1988. 66p.

The Homeless Eligibility Clarification Act of 1986 made it possible for homeless people to use food stamps to obtain meals from authorized providers, and also extended food stamp use to persons in shelters that provide 50 percent or more of their meals. This report examines a variety of topics associated with the use of these laws.

Educational Materials

Educators for Social Responsibility of New York. **Poverty in the United States: Myths and Realities.** New York: Educators for Social Responsibility (425 Riverside Drive, New York, NY 10115), 1987. 20p.

This teaching unit is geared toward use in U.S. history, economics, or social problems courses for high school students. It includes a teacher's manual, background materials, and a quiz for students.

Housing Now! **Housing and Homelessness: A Teaching Guide.** Washington, DC: Housing Now! (425 Second Street, NW, Washington, DC 20001), 1989. 71p.

This curriculum, with lesson plans for both elementary and high school students, examines the background of increased homelessness in the nation and myths about poverty. Affordable housing is explored as a solution to homelessness. The teacher's guide includes a glossary of key terms, as well as a listing of other reading materials and films. The video *Shelter Boy* is included.

Elderly Homeless

Keigher, Sharon M., Rebecca Hanson Berman, and Sadelle Greenblatt. **Relocation, Residence & Risk: A Study of Housing Risks and the Causes of Homelessness among the Urban Elderly.** Chicago: Metropolitan Chicago Coalition on Aging (53 West Jackson Boulevard, Chicago, IL 60604), 1989. 96p. $12.

Gentrification, demolition, and federal cuts in benefits have all contributed to homelessness in the last decade, yet the elderly appear to be underrepresented among the homeless. This report examines the unique housing problems of the older American, as well as the growing shortage of affordable housing.

U.S. Congress. House. Select Committee on Aging. **Homeless Older Americans.** 98th Cong., 2d sess., 1984. 184p.

The number of older people is increasing across the nation, as is the number of homeless people, yet little attention is given to the older homeless person, whose extreme poverty is complicated by poor health, mental difficulties, and greater vulnerability. This hearing examined the physical, mental, and housing needs of the homeless elderly.

Emergency Shelter

Hamberg, Jill. **Building and Zoning Regulations: A Guide for Sponsors of Shelters and Housing for the Homeless in New York City.** New York: Community Service Society (105 East Twenty-second Street, New York, NY 10010), 1984. 49p. $4.

Local regulation often impedes the creation of facilities for the homeless and other groups; although written for a New York City audience, this guide offers a basis for activity anywhere. It presents some of the basic laws covering building and zoning matters, the process of procuring permits and approvals, and issues in site selection.

Housing Assistance Council (HAC). **Rural Emergency Shelter Need.** Washington, DC: Housing Assistance Council (1025 Vermont Avenue, NW, Washington, DC 20005), 1983. 50p. $5.

As homelessness has grown in rural areas—largely due to economic reasons—the need for shelter and services has also expanded in these traditionally underserved areas. This report offers a portrait of the demand for emergency services in sparsely populated areas.

Seldon, Paul, and Margot Jones. **Moving On: Making Room for the Homeless—A Practical Guide to Shelter.** New York: United Church Board for Homeland Ministries, 1982. 63p. $3, from the Coalition for the Homeless.

Setting up a shelter can require a church or community group to obtain zoning permits, notify city agencies, examine other programs, and address community concerns. This manual covers all the basics of "how to" in

New York City, but can easily be applied to other situations, as it also discusses operating procedures, staffing, and funding.

Employment

Barnes, William R., and R. Leo Penne. **Employment Problems and America's Cities.** Washington, DC: National League of Cities, 1984. 99p.

Unemployment and employment at low wages are contributing causes of homelessness, yet monthly unemployment statistics do little to explain the nature of the problem at the local level. This report examines the importance of employment issues to local officials, as well as the problems and priorities these officials identified in a national study.

Shapiro, Isaac, and Marion Nichols. **Unprotected: Unemployment Insurance and Jobless Workers in 1988.** Washington, DC: Center on Budget and Policy Priorities (236 Massachusetts Avenue, NE, Washington, DC 20002), 1989. 20p.

Record cutbacks in unemployment insurance and a sharp increase in long-term unemployment resulted in a record-tying low of only one in three out-of-work Americans receiving unemployment benefits in 1988. This report profiles problems faced by minorities, state efforts, and reductions in training programs.

Southern Regional Council. **Hard Labor: A Report on Day Labor and Temporary Employment.** Atlanta, GA: Southern Regional Council (60 Walton Street, NW, Atlanta, GA 30303), 1988. $10.

Day labor is one of the nation's fastest growing industries, and one easily accessed by many homeless people in need of work. This year-long study looks at day labor in 37 metropolitan areas where poor people do dangerous and difficult work for less than subsistence wages. The report also finds that many agencies routinely violate federal and state antidiscrimination laws.

Food and Hunger

Brown, J. Larry, and H. F. Pizer. **Living Hungry in America.** New York: Macmillan Publishing Company, 1987. 212p. $18.95. ISBN 0-02-517290-5.

In 1985, a team of prominent physicians set out to learn firsthand about hunger in the nation. They toured schools, day care sites, and homes in 19 states, accompanied by other health professionals, social workers, and clergy. This book details the startling extent of the hunger and malnutrition they found.

Food Research and Action Center (FRAC). **Hunger in the Eighties: A Primer.** Washington, DC: Food Research and Action Center, 1984. 166p. $10.

FRAC is the foremost Washington, D.C., organization addressing food-related issues and the poor, and this data-packed examination of hunger issues lays the foundation for examining the nation's commitment to sound food and nutrition policies.

Physician Task Force on Hunger in America. **Hunger in America: The Growing Epidemic.** Middletown, CT: Wesleyan University Press, 1985. 231p. $8.95. ISBN 0-8915-6158-4.

In early 1984, the Physician Task Force, composed of physicians, health experts, and academic and religious leaders, set out to travel the country to document the nature and scope of hunger, much as had been done in New England. Their major findings painted a worsening picture of hunger for the poor.

U.S. Congress. House. Committee on Agriculture. **Review of Nutrition Programs which Assist the Homeless.** 100th Cong., 1st sess., 1987. 337p.

Public officials, shelter providers, and homeless people present their views of how federal nutrition assistance serves the needs of homeless men, women, and children in the streets and in shelters, and also give their opinions on the growing need for emergency food relief.

U.S. Congress. House. Select Committee on Hunger. **Hunger among the Homeless: A Survey of 140 Shelters, Food Stamp Participation and Recommendations.** 100th Cong., 1st sess., 1987. 108p.

Three national organizations working with the homeless surveyed shelters across the country to discover the food assistance needs of the homeless as well as the long-term answers to hunger among the very poor.

Withnell, Elizabeth, Donna V. Porter, and Cathy Gilmore. **Salvaged Food: Background and Analysis.** Washington, DC: Congressional Research Service, Library of Congress, 1982. 65p.

Many local organizations serving the poor and homeless rely on the surplus resources of others to accomplish their work. Foremost among the items discarded in quantity in this country is food. This report examines estimates of wasted food, the development of interest in using this resource, and distribution efforts. A survey of state liability laws is included.

General

American Institute of Architects (AIA). **The Search for Shelter Workbook.** Washington, DC: American Institute of Architects, 1989. $22.

This step-by-step guide is intended to help people become involved effectively in local efforts to end homelessness. It is the most recent product of AIA's Search for Shelter program. A variety of ideas is presented, from raising consciousness in the community, to funding guidelines for homeless programs, to visual materials to aid in organizing.

Appelbaum, Richard P., Peter Drier, Michael Dolny, and John I. Gilderbloom. **Scapegoating Rent Control: Masking the Causes of Homelessness.** Economic Policy Institute Briefing Paper. Washington, DC: Economic Policy Institute, 1730 Rhode Island Avenue, NW, Washington, DC 20036. 27p. $2.

One theory about the cause of homelessness in some cities is that the presence of rent regulation causes landlords not to provide as much affordable housing. This paper refutes the argument of some conservative writers that homelessness and rent regulation are linked.

Bassuk, Ellen L. **"The Homelessness Problem."** *Scientific American,* 251 no. 1 (July 1984): 40–45.

This article received broad coverage for its thesis that many of the homeless are mentally ill people who are not well served by emergency shelters. The author argues that adequate housing and appropriate psychiatric care are necessary to address homelessness.

Baxter, Ellen, and Kim Hopper. **Private Lives/Public Spaces: Homeless Adults on the Streets of New York City.** New York: Community Service Society (105 East Twenty-second Street, New York, NY 10010), 1981. 129p. $6.50.

This 15-month study primarily reports on the causes of contemporary homelessness as they were first revealed in New York and other cities. It describes in detail the procedures and operations of the existing public and private shelters and the ways that homeless persons survive on the streets.

Bevington, Christine Benglia, and Peter Marcuse. **Homelessness and Low-Income Housing: A Working Bibliography.** New York: Architects/

Designers/Planners for Social Responsibility, 1987. 37p. Available from the Coalition for the Homeless.

The nature of homelessness and its major causes, as well as federal and local responses, are covered, as are architecture and design issues associated with creating low-cost housing.

Bingham, Richard D., Roy E. Green, and Sammis B. White, eds. **The Homeless in Contemporary Society.** Beverly Hills, CA: Sage Publications, 1986. 277p. $18.95. ISBN 0-8039-2889-0.

A brief history of homelessness in the United States is presented in this anthology, with essays on veterans, women and children, and the debate over numbers. Attention then turns to the roles of nonprofit and religious organizations; local, state, and federal government roles; and programs in other countries.

Boston Foundation. **Homelessness: Critical Issues for Policy and Practice.** Boston: Boston Foundation, 1987. 64p. $4.

Eleven short essays on homelessness, health, housing, and other topics were prepared for a Boston conference of academics and activists and are presented here as a general overview of the problem.

Cibulskis, Ann M., and Charles Hoch. **Homelessness: An Annotated Bibliography.** Chicago: Council of Planning Librarians (1313 East Sixtieth Street, Chicago, IL 60637), 1986. 32p. $10.

The literature on both traditional homelessness and the homelessness of the early 1980s is covered, with special sections devoted to age-related homelessness, the problems of women, and illness. The listing of area studies and local reports provides a comprehensive base for studying the work of local advocates in assessing the problem.

Cuomo, Mario M. **1933/1983—Never Again.** A Report to the National Governors' Association Task Force on the Homeless. Portland, ME: NGA, 1983. 88p.

This national survey of the problems of hunger and homelessness offers portraits of the needy juxtaposed against the images of the Great Depression. It proposes a national policy for ending homelessness based on adequate emergency relief, improved income and benefits, and federal action to provide permanent housing.

Greer, Nora Richter. **The Creation of Shelter.** Washington, DC: American Institute of Architects (AIA), 1988. 130p. $15.

Specific needs of the homeless in local communities across the nation were the focus of workshops held by the AIA in 1987. This volume documents the results of this effort and includes floor plans for model projects.

————. **The Search for Shelter.** Washington, DC: American Institute of Architects (AIA), 1986. $15.

This resource guide offers an overview of homelessness in the United States as well as 33 case studies of model emergency, transitional, and long-term shelters around the country. The national Search for Shelter program of the AIA took its name from the process involved in this volume, wherein the right to and provision of safe and dignified shelter was explored.

Hamberg, Jill, and Kim Hopper. **The Making of America's Homeless: From Skid Row to New Poor 1945–1984.** New York: Community Service Society (105 East Twenty-second Street, New York, NY 10010), 1984. 91p. $6.50.

A definitive historical perspective on homelessness since World War II, this report offers analyses of poverty and the growing gap between rich and poor, the emergence of widespread homelessness, the impact of de-institutionalization, postwar housing trends, and the development of public programs.

Hope, Marjorie, and James Young. **The Faces of Homelessness.** New York: Lexington Books, 1986. 318p. $15.95. ISBN 0-669-14200-x.

This general view of homelessness includes a national survey of the problem with special focus on Washington, D.C., and Cincinnati. The authors look at the role of displacement, the lack of community supports for the mentally ill, and the problem of unemployment.

Hopper, Kim, Ellen Baxter, Stuart Cox, and Lawrence Klein. **One Year Later: The Homeless Poor in New York City, 1982.** New York: Community Service Society (105 East Twenty-second Street, New York, NY 10010), 1982. 92p. $6.50.

This update on the groundbreaking **Private Lives/Public Spaces** examines the plight of the homeless in New York City one year after the original study.

Interagency Council on the Homeless. **A Nation Concerned: A Report to the President and the Congress on the Response to Homelessness in America.** Washington, DC: Government Printing Office, 1988. 110p.

The Interagency Council is the McKinney-mandated coordinating body of all federal agencies working on the problem of homelessness. The group was initially highly criticized for failing to develop expertise or information resources for those in the field. This report, prepared for

Congress, assesses homelessness and the role volunteer efforts can play in solving it.

Marin, Peter. **"Helping and Hating the Homeless: The Struggle at the Margins of America."** *Harper's* (January 1987): 39–49.

This personal essay on the nature of homelessness and how society reacts to it provides a basic overview of the problem and explores what it means to live on the margins of society. The author also studies the fear created by homelessness and other problems for those who are still better off.

Momeni, Jamshid A., ed. **Homelessness in the United States, Volume I: State Surveys.** Contributions in Sociology No. 73. Westport, CT: Greenwood, 1989. 250p. $49.95. ISBN 0-313-25566-0.

This survey of homelessness across the country contains 14 chapters authored both by individuals and by groups. A wide variety of perspectives is presented; there is no standard data source or analytical method. All attempt to define and solve the problem of homelessness.

Rossi, Peter. **Without Shelter: Homelessness in the 1980s.** New York: Priority Press Publications, 1989. A Twentieth Century Fund paper. 79p. $8.95. ISBN 0-087078-234-7.

This volume examines some of the recent growth of homelessness with a focus on research studies that have attempted to assess the problem.

Schwartz, David C., and John H. Glascock. **Combating Homelessness: A Resource Book.** New Brunswick, NJ: Rutgers University Press, 1989. 178p. $10.

A wide variety of resource materials are presented including recent basic information on homelessness, summaries of federal laws, an overview of funding sources, a listing of state prevention programs, sample statutes, a federal agency contact list, and an extensive bibliography. The information is indexed for easy access.

Sosin, Michael R., Paul Colson, and Susan Grossman. **Homelessness in Chicago: Poverty and Pathology, Social Institutions and Social Change.** Chicago: Chicago Community Trust, 1988. 397p. Free. ISBN 096151180x.

This survey of Chicago homelessness examines social and economic conditions surrounding poverty and finds some characteristics associated with homelessness that appear to be common to all poverty. The report also contains findings about the episodic nature of homelessness for the poor.

Tucker, William. **"America's Homeless: Victims of Rent Control."** The Heritage Foundation *Backgrounder,* No. 685. (January 12, 1989): 1–12.

One theory of why there is a shortage of affordable housing in the cities is that rent regulations reduce the incentive of landlords to create such housing. This paper attempts to link homelessness in certain cities with the presence of rent regulation.

U.S. Conference of Mayors. **A Status Report on Hunger and Homelessness in America's Cities: 1989.** Washington, DC: U.S. Conference of Mayors, 1989. 86p. $10.

The mayors annually survey more than two dozen cities to examine the state of the problems of hunger and homelessness in their communities. They offer profiles of the growth of demand for services, waiting lists for housing, and primary causes of these problems.

U.S. Congress. House. Committee on Banking, Commerce, and Urban Affairs. Subcommittee on Housing and Community Development. **Homelessness in America.** 97th Cong., 2d sess., 1982. 3 volumes. 4,107p.

The highly publicized first congressional hearings on homelessness held since the Great Depression gathered shelter providers, homeless people, and local officials to create a powerful statement of a problem that was not yet widely recognized. The text of these hearings together with the appendices of submitted material are an enduring and detailed record of the nature of homelessness as it began to burst into the national consciousness.

U.S. Department of Housing and Urban Development. **Publications Relating to Homelessness: A Working Bibliography.** HUD Office of Policy and Development Research.

U.S. General Accounting Office (GAO). **Homelessness: A Complex Problem and the Federal Response.** Washington, DC: U.S. General Accounting Office, 1985. 88p. GAO/HRD-85-40.

GAO prepared this study by examining dozens of local, state, and national reports on homelessness; interviewing people working on the issue; and studying federal programs for the homeless. The report enumerates factors affecting homelessness as well as likely long-term strategies for solving the problem.

———. **Welfare Hotels: Uses, Costs, and Alternatives.** Washington, DC: U.S. General Accounting Office, 1989. HRD-89-26BR.

The use of commercial hotels and motels to compensate for the lack of an emergency shelter system in a locality has become a well-known symbol of makeshift efforts to deal with growing homelessness. This government report examines hotels and their services, looking at how much they are used as temporary and permanent housing, rates and how they compare to other types of housing, and possible alternatives.

Health Care

Brickner, Philip, Linda Keen Scharer, Barbara Conanan, Alexander Elvy, and Marianne Savarese, eds. **Health Care of Homeless People.** New York: Springer Publishing Company, 1985. 349p. $29.95. ISBN 0-8261-4990-1.

An overview of health issues for homeless people is presented with special sections on medical disorders, mental health and illness, the organization of health services, and models of health care for the homeless poor. The offerings are by a total of 24 different authors or collaborators with expertise on subjects ranging from infestations to alcoholism to nutrition.

Dowell, Michael, and the National Health Law Program. **State and Local Responsibilities To Provide Medical Care for Indigents.** Chicago: National Clearinghouse for Legal Services (407 South Dearborn, Chicago, IL 60605), 1985. 384p. $25. ISBN 0-941077-02-0. Clearinghouse No. 40,275.

Poor people who are not eligible for Medicaid or Medicare may receive medical care from state or local government. This manual describes the kinds of programs available and provides a state-by-state description of applicable law.

National Association of Community Health Centers. **National Directory of Homeless Health Care Projects.** Washington, DC: National Association of Community Health Centers (1330 New Hampshire Avenue, NW, Washington, DC 20036), 1988. $10.

This directory lists more than 400 organizations providing a variety of health care services in local areas and describes their key services and the target populations they serve.

Rafferty, Margaret, Denise A. Hinzpeter, Laurie Colwin, and Margaret Knox, eds. **The Shelter Worker's Handbook: A Guide for Identifying and Meeting the Health Needs of Homeless People.** New York: Coalition for the Homeless (105 East Twenty-second Street, New York, NY 10010), 1984. 150p. $5.

Life on the streets takes an enormous physical and mental toll on homeless people. Often the most common problems are things unfamiliar to those who volunteer their time in shelters and soup lines: lice and scabies, tuberculosis, psychiatric illness. Understanding the person and understanding the problem must go hand in hand for help to make a difference, and this guide offers basic information by experienced volunteers and professionals.

U.S. Conference of Mayors. **Health Care for the Homeless: A 40-City Review.** Washington, DC: U.S. Conference of Mayors, 1985. 124p. $10.

In late 1984, two major foundations joined the U.S. Conference of Mayors in announcing the results of a competitive grant process: $19.4 million in awards would be distributed to coalitions in 14 of the nation's largest cities for the purpose of providing health care for homeless people. This report provides detailed information from the applications submitted for that process, amounting to a profile of the health needs of homeless people.

Wright, James D. **Health and Homelessness: An Analysis of the Health Status of a Sample of Homeless People Receiving Care through the Department of Community Medicine, St. Vincent's Hospital and Medical Center of New York City: 1969–1984.** Chicago: National Clearinghouse for Legal Services (407 South Dearborn, Chicago, IL 60605), 1985. 122p. $10. Clearinghouse No. 40,229.

The Social and Demographic Research Institute (SDRI) of the University of Massachusetts studied more than 6,000 homeless people receiving health care at one of several health stations located in shelters. This report is the analysis of their findings.

Housing

Apgar, William C., Jr., and H. James Brown. **The State of the Nation's Housing: 1989.** Cambridge: Joint Center for Housing Studies of Harvard University, 1989. 32p. $10.

The late 1980s witnessed an avalanche of housing reports as experts of all sorts sought to analyze the role of the housing market in the growing problem of homelessness. This brief examination of various housing issues looks at homelessness, homeownership, and housing costs.

Bratt, Rachel G., Chester Hartman, and Ann Myerson, eds. **Critical Perspectives on Housing.** Philadelphia: Temple University Press, 1986. 686p. $19.95. ISBN 0-87722-396-3.

This anthology of articles by experts on the structure and economics of the housing market examines a wide variety of housing topics, including the federal, local, and nonprofit roles in providing housing.

Brooks, Mary E. **A Citizen's Guide to Creating a Housing Trust Fund.** San Pedro, CA: Housing Trust Fund Project (570 Shepard Street, San Pedro, CA 90731), 1989. $10.

This handbook explains the basics of housing trust funds and offers case studies of those in Washington and in Boston. Information is offered on how to organize a housing trust fund, including identifying housing needs, assembling a working group, developing a platform, and creating support for the fund.

Brooks, Mary E. **A Survey of Housing Trust Funds.** Washington, DC: Center for Community Change (1000 Wisconsin Avenue, NW, Washington, DC 20007), 1988. 117p. $15.

Housing trust funds are a relatively recent development in the search for resources to build the housing stock. This national survey looks at the basic mechanics of such funds and profiles existing state and local funds across the nation.

Clay, Phillip L. **At Risk of Loss: The Endangered Future of Low-Income Rental Housing Resources.** Washington, DC: Neighborhood Reinvestment Corporation (1325 G Street, NW, Washington, DC 20005), 1987. 51p. $10.

The number of households needing low-rent housing will outpace the total low-rent housing supply by 7.8 million units in the year 2003, if present trends continue and the full potential for loss to the inventory is realized, according to this study. This gap will affect over 18.7 million Americans, who will be without the housing they need.

Community Information Exchange and United Way of America. **Raising the Roof.** 1988. $12.50. 122p. Available from United Way.

This guide to affordable housing strategies in 33 cities across the country covers property acquisition, labor, equipment, financing mechanisms, and community connections.

Council of Large Public Housing Authorities (CLPHA). **Public Housing Today** and **Public Housing Tomorrow.** Boston: Council of Large Public Housing Authorities, 1988. $3 each.

Stereotypes of public housing persist, and these publications offer extensive documentation of who lives in assisted housing, who needs it, what it costs, and what could make it better. Surprising information emerges about this enormous federal resource that serves over 3.5 million people.

Dolbeare, Cushing N. **Out of Reach: Why Everyday People Can't Find Affordable Housing.** Washington, DC: Low Income Housing Information Service (1012 Fourteenth Street, NW, Washington, DC 20005), 1989. 72p. $8.

Detailed information is provided on a state-by-state basis of the gap between the cost of decent housing and what people can afford to pay. Profiles are offered of the gaps faced by persons earning the minimum wage in various housing markets and by renters who rely on public assistance for their income.

Erickson, Jon, and Charles Wilhelm, eds. **Housing the Homeless.** New Brunswick, NJ: Rutgers University Center for Urban Policy Research, 1986. 430p. $19.95. ISBN 0-88285-112-8.

This anthology of articles addresses the political ramifications of homelessness, examining the changing public face of the problem and its many sources. Closer study is given to three groups: the traditional homeless population, the deinstitutionalized mentally ill, and women and children.

Fuchs, Fred. **Introduction to the HUD Public and Subsidized Housing Programs: A Handbook for the Legal Services Advocate.** Chicago: National Clearinghouse for Legal Services (407 South Dearborn, Chicago, IL 60605), 1988. 219p. $25. Clearinghouse No. 43,685.

This guide is an introductory reference to the many federal programs for public and subsidized housing, including conventional public housing, the Section 8 low-income rental assistance programs, the Section 236 Low-Income Rental and Cooperative Housing Program, the Section 221(d)(3) moderate income rental or cooperative housing mortgage insurance program, market interest rate housing, the Section 202 housing for the elderly and handicapped (including people with AIDS), vouchers, and mortgage assistance programs.

Gilderbloom, John, and Richard Appelbaum. **Rethinking Rental Housing.** Philadelphia: Temple University Press, 1988. 280p. $16.95. ISBN 0-87722-538-9.

The authors examine the rental housing crisis as a social issue, not simply an economic one. They examine the possibilities of a national housing program, similar to that of Sweden, with elements of nonprofit community-based housing that gives strong rights to tenants.

Hartman, Chester, ed. **America's Housing Crisis: What Is To Be Done?** Boston: Routledge & Kegan Paul, 1983. 249p. $10.95. ISBN 0-7102-0041-2.

The shortage of affordable housing has made it harder for many homeless people to find their way back from the streets, and more and more of available affordable housing is lost each year. The background of this problem is presented as well as legal strategies to protect low-income units, how the problem relates to the economic crisis of the 1980s, and a look at the burgeoning tenants' movement.

Housing Assistance Council (HAC). **Why Farmers Home Administration Programs Must Be Preserved: The Case for FmHA's Rural Housing, Community Facility, and Farm Programs.** Washington, DC: Housing Assistance Council (1025 Vermont Avenue, NW, Washington, DC 20005), 1985. 72p. $6.50.

The Farmers Home Administration (FmHA) operates rural rental, homeownership, and migrant farmworker housing programs that are the equivalents of HUD programs. FmHA reaches many low-income people through an agency known for local accessibility. This report looks at the vital role these programs play.

Institute for Policy Studies, Working Group on Housing. **The Right to Housing: A Blueprint for Housing the Nation.** Washington, DC: Institute for Policy Studies (1601 Connecticut Avenue, NW, Washington, DC 20009), 1989. 72p. $5. ISBN 0-89758-046-x.

A nationwide group of housing experts produced this paper, which argues that the free market will never meet the housing needs of the low- and moderate-income person. This report provides the basis for a major piece of pending federal housing legislation.

Leonard, Paul A., Cushing N. Dolbeare, and Edward B. Lazere. **A Place To Call Home: The Crisis in Housing for the Poor.** Washington, DC: Center on Budget and Policy Priorities and the Low Income Housing Information Service (236 Massachusetts Avenue, NE, Washington, DC 20002), 1989. 80p. $8.

The first new housing census data in more than four years is extensively analyzed in view of its significant impact on poor Americans. The causes of the housing crisis are examined, as are the special needs of minorities, the elderly, and single parents.

MIT Housing Policy Project Working Papers. Cambridge, MA: MIT Center for Real Estate Development, 1987–1988.

The 20 papers in this series were prepared by housing experts and scholars from across the nation in an effort to analyze housing affordability and quality and the housing market. The papers cover a broad range of issues including an overview of future policy ideas, public housing, the needs of the homeless, preservation, and technical financial concerns.

National Coalition for the Homeless. **Precious Resources: Government-Owned Housing and the Needs of the Homeless.** New York: National Coalition for the Homeless (105 East Twenty-second Street, New York, NY 10010), 1988. 152p. $8.

Finding housing solutions sufficient to meet the needs of the homeless and near-homeless seems a challenging proposition. Yet virtually every community has existing resources—often publicly owned—that are vacant and suitable. This survey of 32 cities around the nation looks at conventional public housing as well as foreclosed properties owned by the federal government, and matches the availability of vacant units with the findings of shelter providers concerning the extent of homelessness in their communities.

National Housing Task Force. **A Decent Place To Live.** Washington, DC: National Housing Task Force (1625 I Street, NW, Washington, DC 20006), 1988. 68p.

The task force, also known as the Rouse-Maxwell Commission, was established in late 1987 as one step in an overarching congressional effort to reexamine national housing policy. More than two dozen persons with national stature in housing policy, production, and finance came together to examine the delivery of housing, financing systems, and the needs of low-income people.

National Low Income Housing Preservation Commission. **Preventing the Disappearance of Low Income Housing.** Report of the National Low Income Housing Preservation Commission to the House Subcommittee on Housing and Community Development and the Senate Subcommittee on Housing and Urban Affairs, United States Congress. 1988. 135p. Free.

This commission was formed as part of the congressional effort to reexamine housing policy in the nation, with an emphasis on the potential loss of subsidized units, the effects of such losses on low-income households, and possible solutions.

Schwartz, David C., Richard C. Ferlauto, and Daniel N. Hoffman. **A New Housing Policy for America: Recapturing the American Dream.** Philadelphia: Temple University Press, 1988. 332p. $19.95. ISBN 0-87722-568-0.

This book's goal is to arrive at a plan to meet U.S. housing needs in the 1990s. The authors examine more than 200 state, national, and international housing efforts.

U.S. Department of Housing and Urban Development (HUD). **Housing America: Freeing the Spirit of Enterprise—A Directory of Official U.S. IYSH Projects.** Washington, DC: HUD Office of Policy Development and Research, 1987. 160p. HUD-1075 PDR.

The United Nations General Assembly designated 1987 as the International Year of Shelter for the Homeless (IYSH). This event was intended to focus world attention and resources on new shelter strategies and policies for the poor. As an official IYSH program, HUD undertook this roster of 166 projects that met its criteria of serving the poor through private sector cooperation with public agencies.

Litigation

Langdon, James K., II, and Mark A. Kass. **"Homelessness in America: Looking for the Right to Shelter."** *Columbia Journal of Law and Social Problems* (1985): 305–392.

Several kinds of state law can provide grounds for establishing an enforceable right to shelter; this article surveys the 50 states and the provisions in their constitutions and general assistance, protective services, and mental health laws.

Legal Services Corporation. **Volunteer Lawyers for the Poor: A Guide to Model Action Programs.** Chicago: National Clearinghouse for Legal Services (407 South Dearborn, Chicago, IL 60605), 1980. 68p. $2.50. Clearinghouse No. 32,493.

Pro bono legal programs have assisted numerous homeless people with a variety of legal problems. This guide explains how to set up such a program, attract volunteer lawyers to it, fund it, and administer it.

National Clearinghouse for Legal Services. **Annotated Case Docket Re: Homeless Litigation.** Chicago: National Clearinghouse Homelessness Task Force (407 South Dearborn, Chicago, IL 60605), 1989. 39p. Clearinghouse No. 40,999. $8.

Litigation is a constantly evolving tool being developed on behalf of the homeless. This narrative overview of cases covers right-to-shelter claims at the state and federal levels, as well as efforts to combat causes of homelessness and the consequences of being homeless, such as the loss of the ability to vote.

O'Connor, Michael A. **Inventory of Legal Services' Initiatives Concerning the Homeless.** Chicago: National Clearinghouse for Legal Services (407 South Dearborn, Chicago, IL 60605), 1985. 26p. $2.50. Clearinghouse No. 39,726.

This report is the result of a survey of advocacy initiatives for the homeless in 19 states. Included are findings on legislation, resolutions, ordinances, conferences, and more. Names of contact persons for the state programs are provided.

McKinney Act

National Coalition for the Homeless. **Necessary Relief: The Stewart B. McKinney Homeless Assistance Act.** New York: National Coalition for the

Homeless (105 East Twenty-second Street, New York, NY 10010), 1988. 38p. $5.

The national coalition maintains a nationwide monitoring network to assess McKinney Act programs at the local level. This evaluation of the programs for 1987–1988 offers program overviews as well as comments by the monitors.

National Governors' Association (NGA). **Status of Programs under the Stewart B. McKinney Homeless Assistance Act and Related Legislation.** Washington, DC: National Governors' Association (444 North Capitol Street, NW, Washington, DC 20001), 1988. 34p. $5.

This summary of McKinney Act programs is part of the NGA effort to monitor the success of the legislation at the state level.

U.S. Conference of Mayors. **A Status Report on the Stewart B. McKinney Homeless Assistance Act of 1987.** Washington, DC: U.S. Conference of Mayors, 1988. 83p. $10.

The McKinney Act provided the first comprehensive federal emergency relief effort for the homeless; this report summarizes the effectiveness of the eight major programs as seen by mayors across the nation.

U.S. Department of Housing and Urban Development. **SAFAH Grants: Aiding Comprehensive Strategies for the Homeless.** Washington, DC: U.S. Government Printing Office, 1988. GPO: 1988 0-225-638: Q: 3. 85p.

A key provision of the McKinney Act is the Supplemental Assistance for Facilities to Assist the Homeless (SAFAH) grants program. Targeted to families with children, the handicapped, and the elderly, SAFAH was designed to fund innovative efforts and to provide a comprehensive service package aimed at self-sufficiency. This report examines 12 of the funded projects.

U.S. General Accounting Office. **Homelessness: Implementation of Food and Shelter Programs under the McKinney Act.** Washington, DC: U.S. General Accounting Office, 1987. 40p. GAO/RCED-88-63.

Several federal programs for the homeless pre-date the 1987 passage of the McKinney Homeless Assistance Act. Both these and the subsequent emergency measures are examined here; numerous possible adjustments in program procedures are offered as well as tables of funding statistics.

———. **HUD's and FEMA's Progress in Implementing the McKinney Act.** Washington, DC: U.S. General Accounting Office, 1989. 136p. GAO/RCED-89-50.

Congress mandated this evaluation of the HUD and FEMA (Federal Emergency Management Association) McKinney programs that provide emergency shelter and various forms of housing assistance. The report not only analyzes the various funding formulas used to disburse money but also profiles grant-receiving agencies and their viewpoints on the causes of the homeless problem.

Mental Illness

Bassuk, Ellen L., ed. **"The Mental Health Needs of Homeless Persons."** *New Directions for Mental Health Services.* Paperback Sourcebook 30. San Francisco: Jossey-Bass, 1986. $14.95. ISBN 0-87589-724-x.

This anthology examines medical, service, and housing needs of mentally ill homeless persons.

Dear, Michael J., and Jennifer R. Wolch. **Landscapes of Despair: From Deinstitutionalizaton to Homelessness.** Princeton, NJ: Princeton University Press, 1987. 220p. $35. ISBN 0-691-07754-1.

Early social welfare institutions in the U.S. are examined in this analysis of the development of large-scale treatment settings for the retarded, the elderly, the mentally disabled, indigents, offenders, and orphans. The significant turn in public policy toward community-based care resulted in massive depopulation of facilities and has been closely linked to homelessness by many writers. The book looks in depth at the case of San Jose, California, and attempts to offer answers for the future development of institutions and land-use tools, such as zoning.

Jaffe, Martin, and Thomas P. Smith. **Siting Group Homes for Developmentally Disabled Persons.** Planning Advisory Service Report No. 397. Chicago: American Planning Association, 1986. 46p. $16.

This report, which includes an annotated bibliography, examines recent literature on the problems of situating community facilities. Overviews of state and local policies and zoning regulations are included, as well as a discussion of legal considerations. Model zoning and fair housing provisions are attached.

Lamb, H. Richard, ed. **The Homeless Mentally Ill.** Washington, DC: American Psychiatric Association (APA), 1984. 280p. $19.95. ISBN 0-89042-200-1.

Many nationally recognized researchers in homelessness and mental illness contributed to APA's position paper on addressing the needs of the homeless mentally ill. This volume incorporates both the medical and social viewpoints of those writers in examining the plight and the needs of the estimated 30 percent of the homeless who suffer from mental illness.

Levine, Adele, ed. **Housing for People with Mental Illness: A Guide for Development.** Princeton, NJ: Robert Wood Johnson Foundation, 1988. 160p. $2.40. Available from Robert Wood Johnson Foundation Program on Chronic Mental Illness, Massachusetts Mental Health Center, 74 Fenwood Road, Boston, MA 02115.

Practical information offered in this volume includes site selection tips, analyzing financial feasibility, choosing a developer, and managing housing.

Sheehan, Susan. **Is There No Place on Earth for Me?** New York: Houghton Mifflin, 1982. 320p. $14.95. ISBN 0-395-31871-8.

This carefully detailed account of the repeated hospitalization and treatment of Sylvia Frumkin, a chronically mentally ill woman in New York, paints a clear and specific portrait of the deficiencies of the public mental health system. Also shown is the toll of mental illness on one family.

Torrey, E. Fuller. **Nowhere To Go: The Tragic Odyssey of the Homeless Mentally Ill.** New York: Harper and Row, 1988. 256p. $18.95. ISBN 0-06-015993-6.

The careless depopulation of public mental hospitals resulted in the creation of Community Mental Health Centers and a vast new federal government structure of ready financing. But the seriously mentally ill, whose plight was supposed to be bettered by these developments, instead were displaced by the "worried well" who sought treatment at these facilities. Compounding the problem, the seriously mentally ill were unable to re-enter hospitals because of recently tightened admissions standards.

Torrey, E. Fuller, and Sidney M. Wolfe. **Care of the Seriously Mentally Ill: A Rating of State Programs.** Washington, DC: Public Citizen Health Research Group (2000 P Street, NW, Washington, DC 20036), 1986. 105p.

A state-by-state profile of services for the seriously mentally ill examines the quality of care provided by the state agencies that have historically been responsible for the treatment and rehabilitation of those in need.

Torrey, E. Fuller, Eve Bargmann, and Sidney Wolfe. **Washington's Grate Society: Schizophrenics in the Shelters and on the Street.** Washington, DC: Public Citizen Health Research Group (2000 P Street, NW, Washington, DC 20036), April 1985. 23p.

Perhaps no homeless people are as visible as those who exhibit signs of severe mental illness in public places; few shelter residents are more disruptive than those whose illness is untreated or unrecognized. This survey of public shelters in Washington, D.C., found that 39 percent of the residents suffered from schizophrenia and that this was the primary reason for their homelessness. The report also contains significant findings about the prevalence of illness among those not in shelters.

U.S. Conference of Mayors. **Local Responses to the Needs of Homeless Mentally Ill Persons.** Washington, DC: U.S. Conference of Mayors, 1987. 66p. $10.

The Conference of Mayors and the National Institute of Mental Health convened a series of meetings to examine homeless mentally ill persons and their unique needs. The case studies presented in this volume focus on housing, services, daytime centers, education of public safety officials, and coordination of services.

U.S. General Accounting Office. **Homeless Mentally Ill: Problems and Options in Estimating Numbers and Trends.** Washington, DC: U.S. General Accounting Office, August 1988. 122p. GAO/PEMD-88-24.

This report tries to analyze the various methods attempted to date to count the homeless mentally ill and concludes that there is no sound national estimate. Although it is a rather technical examination of existing research methods, this analysis does offer a summary chart of the previous counting efforts.

Minorities

Housing Assistance Council (HAC). **A Catalog of Information Sources on Rural Housing and Poverty.** Washington, DC: Housing Assistance Council (1025 Vermont Avenue, NW, Washington, DC 20005), 1985. 39p. $4.25.

————. **Losing Ground: Public Policy and the Displacement of Rural Black-Owned Homesteads.** Washington, DC: Housing Assistance Council (1025 Vermont Avenue, NW, Washington, DC 20005), 1984. 78p. $7.

Homelessness in rural areas takes very different forms from that seen in city streets. Consequently, it also requires different solutions. This report looks at the impact of recent public policy on poor minority residents of rural areas.

————. **Population, Poverty and Housing Conditions of American Indians, Eskimos, and Aleuts: 1980.** Washington, DC: Housing Assistance Council (1025 Vermont Avenue, NW, Washington, DC 20005), 1985. 131p. $11.

Poverty is an enduring problem for many native populations in the U.S. While homelessness takes a different identity in cultural groups for whom the extended family is still a strong unit, housing problems and conditions are a major factor linked to the poverty prevalent in native populations. The groups covered in this report are among the major populations targeted by recent federal programs for the homeless.

————. **Who Will House Farmworkers? An Examination of State Programs.** Washington, DC: Housing Assistance Council (1025 Vermont Avenue, NW, Washington, DC 20005), 1986. 43p. $4.50.

Rural agricultural areas face homelessness and housing problems directly tied to the economy of migrant farmworkers. This report explores state programs attempting to assist this population, which is generally composed of poor and minority people.

Lazere, Edward B., and Paul A. Leonard. **The Crisis in Housing for the Poor: A Special Report on Hispanics and Blacks.** Washington, DC: Center on Budget and Policy Priorities (236 Massachusetts Avenue, NE, Washington, DC 20002), 1989. 39p.

Recent census information shows that Hispanics and blacks are more likely to be poor than whites, and thus they face even more difficult burdens in meeting the rising cost of housing. This paper examines the market faced by minorities, including the condition of housing available to them.

Model Programs

Public Technology, Inc. **Caring for the Hungry and Homeless: Exemplary Programs.** Washington, DC: Public Technology, Inc. (1301 Pennsylvania Avenue, NW, Washington, DC 20004), 1985. 135p. $10.

The National Board of the Emergency Food and Shelter Program commissioned this report, which profiles 50 food, shelter, and supportive service programs around the country. The programs range from emergency shelter and food banks to job training and health care.

U.S. Department of Health and Human Services. **Helping the Homeless: A Resource Guide.** Washington, DC: U.S. Department of Health and Human Services, 1984. 204p. GPO 1984 0-454-738.

Emergency feeding programs, emergency shelters, transitional housing, long-term housing, and multiservice programs are profiled. Special sections are provided on sources of funding and food; facilities and equipment; licensing, laws, and regulations; program design and operations;

and common questions and answers on administrative and structural issues. An appendix explains how to seek government assistance.

Photography

Hollyman, Stephenie. **We the Homeless: Portraits of America's Displaced People.** Text by Victoria Irwin of the *Christian Science Monitor.* New York: Philosophical Library, 1988. 256p. $45. ISBN 0-8022-2542-x.

For more than a year, photographer Stephenie Hollyman traveled around the U.S., meeting and photographing homeless people. Her 15,000-mile trek resulted in these pictures of homeless families and their children, Vietnam veterans, the chronically mentally ill, and the many others who populate the nation's streets and shelters.

National Mental Health Association and Families for the Homeless. **Homeless in America.** Washington, DC: Acropolis Books, 1988. 150p. $19.95. ISBN 0-87491-904-5.

Under the auspices of this joint public education project, some of the best known photojournalists in the nation created images of the homeless with the goal of raising public awareness. This resulting volume was issued in conjunction with an exhibit of the photos, which toured the nation until 1990.

Poverty

Center on Budget and Policy Priorities. **Holes in the Safety Net: Poverty Programs and Policies in the States.** Washington, DC: Center on Budget and Policy Priorities (236 Massachusetts Avenue, NE, Washington, DC 20002), 1988. $8 (national report); $3.50 (state reports).

Federal policies and programs affecting poor people are examined in the national overview; the individual state reports portray how residents fare under general assistance, food stamps, medical assistance, in the housing market, and more.

Harrington, Michael. **The New American Poverty.** New York: Penguin Books, 1985. 255p. $7.95. ISBN 0-14-008112-7.

From the author who wrote the eye-opening *The Other America,* which is credited with starting the War on Poverty, comes this volume on poverty in the 1980s. Noteworthy is the section devoted to a discussion of the use of numbers in counting the poor and assessing their poverty.

Housing Assistance Council (HAC). **Rural Housing and Poverty in the United States: An Analysis of Census Data.** Washington, DC: Housing Assistance Council (1025 Vermont Avenue, NW, Washington, DC 20005), 1985. 28p. $8.50.

Rural housing problems are substantially different from those found in urban settings; poverty may be more deeply entrenched. Because services are more difficult to provide in rural areas and more scarce for those in need, this assessment of census indicators of rural shelter and poverty problems offers a clear picture of the barriers faced in assisting the rural poor.

National League of Cities (NLC). **Poverty in America: New Data, New Perspectives.** Washington, DC: NLC, 1987. 12p. ISBN 0-933729-19-7.

This analysis of 1985 census data on poverty includes metropolitan and non-metropolitan information as well as a special focus on the working poor.

Prevention

Gillett, Robert F. **Foreclosure Prevention Programs Available to Homeowners with Governmentally Insured Mortgages.** Chicago: National Clearinghouse for Legal Services (407 South Dearborn, Chicago, IL 60605), 1985. 13p. $1.75. Clearinghouse No. 40,251.

One of the best homelessness prevention programs is to keep a person who is already housed in that housing even after a crisis arises in daily life. Several programs exist for those who reside in homes with mortgages backed by the federal government. This guide explains how to use the programs to assist persons who are at risk.

Homebase/Regional Support Center for Homelessness Policy and Programs. **Breaking the Link between Eviction and Homelessness: An Eviction Prevention Plan.** San Francisco: Homebase (1535 Mission Street, San Francisco, CA 94103), 1989. 50p. $4.

This study of intervention methods in the eviction-homelessness cycle examines the possibilities of emergency financial aid for tenants with back rent problems as well as necessary information services for those at risk, including legal representation and a hotline. Ways the legal system could be changed in behalf of tenants and possible long-term prevention efforts are also explored.

Lofquist, William A. **Discovering the Meaning of Prevention: A Practical Approach to Positive Change.** Tucson: AYD Publications (P.O. Box 36748, Tucson, AZ 85740), 1983. 151p. $10. ISBN 0-913951-00-5.

Asserting that prevention is "an active, assertive process of creating conditions... that promote the well-being of people," this volume explores ways the individual and the community can tackle social problems, assess their progress in achieving change, and build support systems for the future.

Rights of the Homeless

Citizens' Commission on Civil Rights, National Center for Policy Alternatives. **Barriers to Registration and Voting: An Agenda for Reform.** Washington, DC: Citizens' Commission on Civil Rights, 1987. 171p. ISBN 0-89788-095-1.

Once homeless, people also easily lose a number of other intangibles. Among these has often been the right to vote, lost because local laws are interpreted to require that one have a permanent residence in order to exercise the franchise. Beginning in 1984, a number of local efforts around the country attempted to alleviate this problem. This report, the product of three hearings around the nation, includes information on barriers faced by homeless persons.

Mental Health Law Project. **Federal and State Rights and Entitlements of People Who Are Homeless.** Chicago: National Clearinghouse for Legal Services (407 South Dearborn, Chicago, IL 60605), 1987, 1988.

The Mental Health Law Project prepared several state-specific guides to rights and entitlements for homeless people. People working with the homeless will find these guides useful in helping to obtain welfare rights, income assistance, housing, food and nutrition aid, health care, and veterans' services.

Practising Law Institute. **The Rights of the Homeless 1988.** New York: Practising Law Institute (810 Seventh Avenue, New York, NY 10019), 1988. 624p. $50. H4-5059, PLI. Litigation and Administrative Practice Series (Litigation Course Handbook Series Number 366; Chairman, Robert M. Hayes).

PLI has annually presented a one-day course for attorneys and others working with the homeless on current developments in the application of the rights of the homeless. This volume, from the 1988 course, covers emergency assistance rights, the right to vote, right to treatment for the mentally ill, the prevention of homelessness, and other legal cases. The volume includes decisions and pleadings from some of the cases.

Rural Homelessness

Housing Assistance Council (HAC). **Homelessness from a Rural Perspective.** Washington, DC: Housing Assistance Council (1025 Vermont Avenue, NW, Washington, DC 20005), 1987. 42p. $4.50.

Homelessness in rural areas takes different forms from that in other settings. It is much less visible, services are less available, and poverty is often more entrenched. This report explains some of the unique dimensions of homelessness in rural areas.

Salerno, Dan, Kim Hopper, and Ellen Baxter. **Hardship in the Heartland: Homelessness in Eight U.S. Cities.** New York: Community Service Society (105 East Twenty-second Street, New York, NY 10010), 1984. 184p. $10.

This well-documented report looks at the growth of homelessness in Cleveland, Tulsa, Chicago, Denver, Detroit, Milwaukee, Cincinnati, and Madison, providing a summary of existing research efforts and a specific examination of the mentally ill homeless.

Single Room Occupancy (SRO) Housing

Baxter, Ellen. **The Heights: A Community Housing Strategy.** New York: Community Service Society (105 East Twenty-second Street, New York, NY 10010), 1986. 69p. $6.50.

The author, who conducted some of the groundbreaking research on New York homelessness, has completed a series of supportive SRO facilities in the Washington Heights section of New York City, financed by a combination of public and private resources. This report describes in detail the steps necessary to achieve this model of housing for previously homeless people.

Central City Concern. **SRO Housing Management Handbook.** Portland, OR: Central City Concern (222 N.W. Couch Street, Portland, OR 97209), 1988. $25.

Central City Concern, a major SRO developer in Portland, created this handbook, which describes general management procedures for facilities, accounting operations, and tenant relations.

Coalition for the Homeless. **Single Room Occupancy Hotels: Standing in the Way of the Gentry.** New York: Coalition for the Homeless (105 East Twenty-second Street, New York, NY 10010), 1985. 82p. $8.

Single room occupancy hotels (SROs) are one of the last remaining traditional sources of low-cost rental housing in urban areas. Hundreds of thousands of these units have been demolished in the last decade as downtown centers have been leveled and redeveloped with convention centers, new luxury hotels, and office complexes. This paper, produced jointly with the SRO Tenants Rights Coalition, examines this problem in New York City, as well as available tenant protections and legal avenues to avoid building conversions.

SRO Housing Corporation, Inc. **Single Room Occupancy Development Handbook.** Los Angeles: SRO Housing Corporation (311 South Spring Street, Los Angeles, CA 90013), 1987. 40p. $14.50.

The development of an SRO facility is examined with accompanying sample layouts for space, income calculations, and a checklist for managers.

Werner, Frances E., and David Bryson. **"A Guide to the Preservation and Maintenance of Single Room Occupancy (SRO) Housing."** *Clearinghouse Review,* vol. 15, no. 12 (1981): 999–1009; vol. 16, no. 1 (1982): 1–25. Chicago: National Clearinghouse for Legal Services (407 South Dearborn, Chicago, IL 60605). $6 each.

This series of articles is a comprehensive guide for local organizations and legal activists seeking to preserve SRO hotels as a low-cost housing form.

State Programs

The American Federation of State, County, and Municipal Employees (AFSCME), AFL-CIO. **The Republican Record: A 7-Year Analysis of State Losses of Federal Funding (FY 1982–FY 1988).** Washington, DC: AFSCME, 1988. 225p.

Federal domestic spending was drastically altered under the Reagan administration. This program-by-program, state-by-state analysis of those cuts examines not only the individual entitlements and benefits, but also the programs that provide aid to state and local governments, summing up per capita effects of the cuts for each state.

The Council of State Housing Agencies. **Housing Initiatives of State Housing Finance Agencies.** Washington, DC: The Council of State Housing Agencies (444 North Capitol Street, NW, Washington, DC 20001), 1987. 94p. $15.

This overview of housing programs at the state level examines initiatives ranging from rental assistance programs to trust funds.

Nenno, Mary, ed. **Assistance for Homeless Persons: A NAHRO Resource Book for Housing and Community Development Officials.** Washington, DC: National Association of Housing and Redevelopment Officials (NAHRO) (1320 Eighteenth Street, NW, Washington, DC 20036), 1988. 143p.

Federal programs for the homeless are summarized along with state efforts in legislation, programs linking housing and human services, and other resources. Selected state programs are presented in more depth, as are statutes and case studies of local agency work.

Nenno, Mary K., and George Colyer. **New Money and New Methods: A Catalog of State and Local Initiatives in Housing and Community Development.** Washington, DC: National Association of Housing and Redevelopment Officials (NAHRO) (1320 Eighteenth Street, NW, Washington, DC 20036), 1988. 106p. $25.

This collection of articles, reports, and case studies examines public and private initiatives to assist housing.

Sidor, John, and Horace Barker. **State Housing Initiatives: The 1988 Compendium.** Washington, DC: Council of State Community Affairs Agencies (COSCAA) (444 North Capitol Street, Washington, DC 20001), 1988. 132p.

State financial aid for all sorts of housing programs exists, but often agencies or community organizations do not know how to seek it out. This reference book covers programs ranging from new construction to housing for special needs.

The Urban Institute. **State Activities and Programs for the Homeless: A Review of Six States.** Washington, DC: The Urban Institute, 1988. 140p.

As homelessness has increased around the nation and federal dollars have proved inadequate to solve the problem, some states have undertaken their own initiatives. This survey for the Interagency Council on the Homeless covers California, Connecticut, Georgia, New Mexico, Ohio, and Wisconsin, and offers a look at efforts to implement an entire range of programs to address homelessness.

Technical Assistance

Carter, Nicala. **Resources for Nonlawyers.** Chicago: National Clearinghouse for Legal Services, 1985. 14p. Available free from the clearinghouse (407 South Dearborn, Chicago, IL 60605).

This annotated bibliography is reprinted from a special issue on advocacy for the poor. It includes a useful list of resources for the nonlawyer who needs information on legal issues, is seeking to help a poor person with a legal situation, or wishes to more actively engage the legal system as an advocate.

Coalition on Human Needs. **The National Technical Assistance Directory: A Guide for State Advocates and Service Providers.** Washington, DC: Coalition on Human Needs, 1989. 47p. $10.

Summaries of organizational activity, publications, and available technical assistance are provided for major groups working on poverty issues.

Shelter Development Project. **Financial Management Systems for Shelter for the Homeless. Part One: The Bookkeeping and Financial Reporting System.** 91p. **Part Two: Financial Planning and Control Systems.** 88p. New York: Community Service Society (105 East Twenty-second Street, New York, NY 10010), 1985. $6.50 each.

This set of advanced handbooks for shelter providers offers the basics in implementing necessary accounting and reporting systems for shelter programs.

Transitional Facilities

Sprague, Joan F. **A Manual on Transitional Housing.** Boston: Women's Institute for Housing and Economic Development, 1986. 48p. $10.

Emergency shelter can solve various immediate needs, but many homeless people need a next step before permanent housing and any effort at independent living. Transitional housing has been seen to fill this need by providing supportive services, a period for training, and a concrete time for building self-sufficiency. This manual offers definitions of this sort of housing, program options, a guide to development, models, and tips on operating a transitional program.

Veterans

City of New York. **Soldiers of Misfortune: Homeless Veterans in New York City.** New York: Research and Liaison Unit, Office of the Comptroller, City of New York, 1982. 19p. $3.

Veterans are estimated to represent about one-third of the homeless population. This brief report about male veterans in New York City examines factors causing homelessness among veterans, failure of the Veterans Administration to reach out to this population, and programs that could help.

Veterans Administration. **Programs To Assist Homeless Veterans.** Washington, DC: U.S. Government Printing Office, January 1989. 129p. Free.

This comprehensive listing of federal programs with provisions affecting homeless veterans offers a wide range of resources for the needs of homeless veterans. Presented are services ranging from domiciliary care for mentally ill veterans to housing loans and counseling services.

Welfare

Coalition on Human Needs. **The Family Support Act: An Early Implementation Guide.** Washington, DC: Coalition on Human Needs, 1989. 101p.

The Family Support Act, passed in 1988, offers the opportunity for states to assist welfare recipients out of poverty through the use of the new JOBS (Job Opportunities and Basic Skills) program. This manual, directed at advocates and community organizations, covers work, education, and job training activities as well as related child care and health care issues.

Newman, Sandra J., and Ann B. Schnare. **Subsidizing Shelter: The Relationship between Welfare and Housing Assistance.** Part 1: Analysis and Findings; Part 2: Data Book. Washington, DC: The Urban Institute Press, 1988. 193p. $8. ISBN 0-87766-414-5.

Welfare recipients receive at least $10 billion annually for housing assistance, funds that are part of their public assistance benefits. The HUD stream of funding for low-income housing is about the same, yet the relationship between the two programs is largely unexamined and their effects uncoordinated.

U.S. General Accounting Office. **Welfare Simplification: States' Views on Coordinating Services for Low-Income Families.** Washington, DC: U.S. General Accounting Office, July 1987. 93p. GAO/HRD-87-110FS.

Homeless or housed, the poor person seeking assistance through public programs faces an array of confusing and often entangled jurisdictions and requirements. This study of access to and use of benefits at the state level examines the major programs—including Aid to Families with Dependent Children (AFDC), Medicaid, food stamps, emergency assistance, and Section 8 low-income housing—for possibilities and problems associated with integrated and improved service delivery, which is commonly referred to as one-stop shopping.

Women

Birch, Eugenie Ladner, ed. **The Unsheltered Woman: Women and Housing in the 80's.** New Brunswick, NJ: Rutgers University Center for Urban Policy Research, 1985. 313p. $14.95. ISBN 0-88285-104-7.

This is a collection of 20 essays on women and their housing needs that were prepared as an overview of necessary shelter and support services for a joint program of the Ford Foundation and Hunter College.

Hirsch, Kathleen. **Songs from the Alley.** New York: Ticknor & Fields, 1989. 420p. $22.95. ISBN 0-89919-488-5.

The lives of two homeless women in Boston—Wendy and Amanda—are traced from their beginnings to the harsh everyday life of homelessness. In an unusual format, this account runs side by side with a review of aid to the homeless poor during the 200 years of Massachusetts' history, including recent political activism for the homeless.

Koegel, Paul. **Ethnographic Perspectives on Homeless and Homeless Mentally Ill Women.** Proceedings of a workshop held October 30–31, 1986, at the National Institute of Mental Health in Rockville, MD. 77p.

This research-oriented conference explored the process by which women become homeless, their social support networks, mental health issues, and women's relations with mental health service providers. It concludes with recommendations for further research and improvements in service delivery.

Rousseau, Ann Marie, and Alix K. Shulman. **Shopping Bag Ladies: Homeless Women Talk about Their Lives.** New York: Pilgrim Press, 1982. 160p. $9.95. ISBN 0-8298-0603-2.

This book of photographs depicts some of the rigors of life for homeless women in New York City. Some women tell their own stories and the homeless are shown in all aspects of their daily routine.

Watson, Sophie. **Housing and Homelessness: A Feminist Perspective.** London and Boston: Routledge & Kegan Paul, 1986. 186p. $14.95. ISBN 0-7102-0400-0.

Although written from the viewpoint of British society, this is a worthwhile study of how Western society in general defines and provides for housing needs, with a particular emphasis on the impact of these policies on women.

Youth

Citizen's Committee for Children and the Coalition for the Homeless Runaway and Homeless Youth Advocacy Program. **Homeless Youth in New York City: Nowhere To Turn.** New York: Coalition for the Homeless (105 East Twenty-second Street, New York, NY 10010), 1983. 25p. $4.

This assessment of the assistance and services available to the ever-increasing numbers of homeless youth in New York City underscores the need for comprehensive policies to aid this population.

The William T. Grant Foundation Commission on Work, Family, and Citizenship. **The Forgotten Half: Pathways to Success for America's Youth and Young Families: Final Report.** Washington, DC: The William T. Grant Foundation (1001 Connecticut Avenue, NW, Washington, DC 20036), 1988. 203p. Single copies free.

Approximately 20 million Americans ages 16 to 24 will not go on to college. This report examines the demographic facts about their lives, including the growth of poverty in this group, the decline of marriage rates, housing affordability problems, health needs, and employment prospects. There are special examinations of the chronically poor, youth at risk, rural youth, youth in foster care, and runaways.

9

Nonprint Resources

Databases

COMSEARCH Foundation Funding
Source: The Foundation Center
               1001 Connecticut Avenue, NW
               Washington, DC 20036
               (800) 424-9836
Cost: Variable

Computerized database searches can be performed to locate foundations that provide support for specific subject area or geographic area efforts. Four major categories for which printouts are available: broad topics ($38), including health care, families, children, services; subjects ($18), for program areas such as health care, volunteer programs, rural issues; geographic ($30), providing an analysis by region or states receiving the greatest share of funds; special topics ($18), including the most frequently requested foundation listings.

Federal Funds Information for States (FFIS)
Source: National Conference of State Legislatures (NCSL)
               1050 Seventeenth Street, Suite 2100
               Denver, CO 80265
               (303) 623-7800
Cost: Annual subscription basis

NCSL operates this database jointly with the National Governors' Association. Detailed computerized information and projections are available on about 90 percent of the federal funds being distributed in each state, for more than 240 programs. Subscribers receive three reports annually under the service.

HandsNet

Source: HandsNet
303 Potrero Street, Suite 54
Santa Cruz, CA 40842
(408) 427-0808

Cost: $25 monthly, plus one-time fee for software and fees for online time

System: Macintosh, IBM PCs

This national computer network of advocates for the hungry and homeless includes many state coalitions as well as key research organizations. The project was originally developed under grants from Apple Computer and USA for Africa/Hands Across America, which provide the technology and training for the system. Groups can access daily news briefs, post inquiries or news on policy issues, scan federal regulation updates, and use electronic mail to communicate rapidly on a 24-hour basis.

HUD USER

Source: HUD USER
P.O. Box 6091
Rockville, MD 20850
(800) 245-2691

Cost: $10 (standard); $20 (custom)

Standard searches on housing topics are available from the online services of the Department of Housing and Urban Development. Standard search topics include federal housing assistance programs, Community Development Block Grants, affordable housing, and housing for the elderly. Custom searches are also performed for other up-to-date information.

LEGISNET

Source: National Conference of State Legislatures
1050 Seventeenth Street, Suite 2100
Denver, CO 80265
(303) 623-7800

Cost: None

This system abstracts thousands of legislative research reports, public policy documents, state surveys, and statistical information. The database is available for all state legislators and their staff to query.

Local Government Information Network (LOGIN)

Source: National League of Cities (NLC)
1301 Pennsylvania Avenue, NW
Washington, DC 20004
(202) 626-3000

Cost: Various subscription packages

System: Almost any personal computer, word processor, or data
               terminal

Local officials can communicate with their colleagues via this system, as
well as access a 25,000-unit database on local government programs.
Services are provided for both large and small communities.

Local Information Network for Universal Service (LINUS)

Source: National League of Cities (NLC)
               1301 Pennsylvania Avenue, NW
               Washington, DC 20004
               (202) 626-3000

Cost: Actual time used

System: Almost any personal computer, word processor, or data
               terminal

Local officials can access all information offered by the NLC, the International City Management Association, and their counterparts in other
jurisdictions, as well as services provided by some participating public
interest groups.

National Clearinghouse on Alcohol Information (NCALI) Database

Source: NCALI Database Search Service
               P.O. Box 2345
               Rockville, MD 20852
               (301) 468-2600

Cost: None

Annotated references from over 200 alcohol-related information sources
are available through this service. Custom searches are performed for
subjects, authors, key words, or year of publication.

National League of Cities Database

Source: National League of Cities (NLC)
               1301 Pennsylvania Avenue, NW
               Washington, DC 20004

Cost: Subscription

Customized printouts of various databases about city officials and cities are
available through this service. The City Officials Data Base provides contact information on mayors, council members, and selected department
heads; individual terms of office are available for some officials. The City
Information Data Base offers facts on government structure, elections,
terms of office, and the jurisdiction itself. City information is available for
all cities over 10,000 population, and for smaller cities if they belong to the
NLC.

National Resource Center on Homelessness and Mental Illness Database
Source: Policy Research Associates, Inc.
                 262 Delaware Avenue
                 Delmar, NY 12054
                 (800) 444-7415
Cost: Variable

Both standard and customized bibliographic searches are available from this database, covering dual diagnosis, epidemiology, ethnographic research, families and children, general issues, health and health care, housing, legal issues, and outreach.

Volunteer Opportunities
Source: National Volunteer Clearinghouse for the Homeless
                 425 Second Street, NW
                 Washington, DC 20001
                 1-800-HELP-664
Cost: Free printout

This database, a project of the Community for Creative Non-Violence, lists volunteer opportunities across the nation for people who want to help the homeless through food, shelter, medical services, and more. Interested persons request a listing for their area and receive a printout.

Films and Videocassettes

The AIDS Movie
Type: 16mm film, video
Length: 26 min.
Cost: Purchase $390, rental $57
Source: Durrin Productions
                 1748 Kalorama Road, NW
                 Washington, DC 20009
                 (202) 387-6700
Date: 1989

Three people with AIDS talk about what it's like to have the disease. An AIDS educator discusses awareness and prevention needs in the community.

Back Wards to Back Streets
Type: Video
Length: 55 min.
Cost: Purchase $445, rental $75

Source: Filmakers Library
              124 East Fortieth Street
              New York, NY 10016
              (212) 808-4980
Date: 1981

Efforts to reintegrate former mental patients into the community are largely regarded as unsuccessful, inadequate, and a major contributing factor to homelessness. This investigative report, directed by Roger Weisberg for Public Policy Productions, looks at some successful community treatment programs, but also at the failures that resulted for the deinstitutionalized patient, including examinations of adult homes, the need for social services, and homelessness.

Both Sides of the Street
Type: 16mm film, video
Length: 18 min.
Cost: Purchase $300 (film), $175 (video);
              rental $70 (film), $55 (video)
Source: Onewest Media
              P.O. Box 5766
              Santa Fe, NM 87502
              (505) 983-8685
Date: 1986

The Tenderloin area of San Francisco is under pressure from development that threatens many of the older and working residents, as well as the homeless and runaways who seek refuge there. Barbara Neal directed this film, which tells one woman's story as she sees her neighborhood change.

Down and Out in America
Type: Video
Length: 60 min.
Source: Joseph Fuery Productions
              200 West Eighty-sixth Street #11A
              New York, NY 10024
              (212) 877-7700
Date: 1986

Lee Grant directed this Academy Award–winning portrayal of the stories of people suffering from job loss, farm foreclosures, lack of housing, and other problems. Told through powerful interviews, the film examines the Los Angeles "Justiceville" encampment of the homeless as well as the notorious welfare hotels of New York City.

The Fall of the I Hotel
Type: 16mm film, video
Length: 57 min.

Cost:	Purchase $650 (film), $250 (video);
	rental $100 (film), $70 (video)
Source:	Onewest Media
	P.O. Box 5766
	Santa Fe, NM 87502
	(505) 983-8685

San Francisco's International Hotel was demolished in 1977 after an eight-year struggle by hotel residents, neighborhood churches, organized labor, and senior citizen groups. For several decades, the hotel had provided low-cost housing to many immigrant Filipinos, the last of whom waged an unsuccessful battle against developers who sought to build a parking garage on the site. This award-winning film combines interviews with residents, news footage, and other resources to tell its story, culminating with the forcible removal of the last tenants.

Food Not Bombs

Type:	Video
Length:	25 min.
Cost:	Purchase $20
Source:	Haight-Ashbury Free TV
	1827 Haight Street #201
	San Francisco, CA 94117
	(414) 995-2397
Date:	1988

The Food Not Bombs organization had 92 of its volunteers arrested by police for serving free food to homeless people. This film documents the struggle between local authorities and members of the community.

Footage Sampler: Homelessness, the Unseen Dimensions

Type:	Video
Length:	21 min.
Cost:	Negotiable
Source:	Julia Keydel
	Homelessness Videotape Project
	131 West 87th Street, No. 1B
	New York, NY 10024
Date:	1983

Through interviews, this film examines the controversy generated in an Upper West Side neighborhood by a proposal to expand outreach services for the homeless through the creation of a referral center. Homeless people and other community residents, as well as workers at the Goddard-Riverside Project Reach-Out program, are featured in this work, which was directed by Julia Keydel. The video shows the homeless on a human level and depicts solutions to the problems faced in the community.

Girltalk

Type:	Video
Length:	55 min.
Cost:	Rental $75
Source:	Filmakers Library
	124 East Fortieth Street
	New York, NY 10016
	(212) 808-4980
Date:	1989

The troubled lives of three teenage girls are depicted, showing virtually the entire range of problems faced by the young poor, problems that can all too easily result in homelessness. The subjects are young veterans of juvenile courts, marginal jobs, foster homes, and teen pregnancy.

God Bless the Child

Type:	Video
Length:	96 min.
Cost:	Home video rental
Source:	Local video stores
Date:	1988

A single working mother is displaced from her home and can find no affordable housing. Homeless, she loses her job and takes her child out of school. She is helped by an outreach worker, only to have her daughter suffer rat bites and lead paint poisoning in the rundown house they rent. Evicted, she makes the decision to abandon her child to foster care.

Hard Drugs

Type:	16mm film, video
Length:	16 min.
Cost:	Purchase $325 (film), $200 (video); rental $50
Source:	The Cinema Guild
	1697 Broadway
	New York, NY 10019
	(212) 246-5522
Date:	1976

In this documentary, drug addicts talk about what led them to use drugs. People working to help the addicts are also interviewed.

Heroism

Type:	Video
Length:	28 min.
Cost:	Purchase $250, rental $50
Source:	The Cinema Guild
	1697 Broadway
	New York, NY 10019
	(212) 246-5522

Date: 1987

An examination of some of the many people and organizations that have come together to offer services for people with AIDS (PWAs) in San Francisco. PWAs talk about how they help each other, and volunteer meal providers, artists, and medical researchers discuss their roles.

Home

Type: Video
Length: 28 min.
Cost: Purchase $295, rental $50
Source: The Cinema Guild
               1697 Broadway
               New York, NY 10019
               (212) 246-5522
Date: 1986

A group of squatters in Brooklyn is the focus of this film, which documents the crisis of affordable housing in the nation and the possible solution offered by those reclaiming abandoned city-owned properties. Members of ACORN, a group that advocates squatting, and community leaders are interviewed about the controversy over this tactic.

Homeless in America

Type: Video
Length: 12 min.
Cost: Purchase $29.50
Source: National Mental Health Association (NMHA)
               1021 Prince Street
               Alexandria, VA 22314
               (703) 684-7722
Date: 1988

Portions of the major national traveling exhibit on homelessness, assembled by the NMHA and Families for the Homeless, are presented. Some of the nation's most prominent photographers participated in this project to show the human side of homelessness.

Homeless in Philadelphia

Type: Video
Length: 48 min.
Cost: Purchase $210, rental $50
Source: Circulating Film Library Museum of Modern Art
               11 West 53rd Street
               New York, NY 10019
               (212) 708-9530
Date: 1986

The Committee for Dignity and Fairness for the Homeless sponsored this film; homeless people helped plan and produce the story, which depicts those homeless who are ready, willing, and able to work and speak out for themselves.

Housekeeping

Type: Video
Length: 117 min.
Cost: Home video rental
Source: Local video stores
Date: 1987

Two teenage girls in the Northwest wind up being cared for by their aunt, who has been riding freight trains. Though the aunt, played by Christine Lahti, tries hard, she has brought with her the ways of the road, including insulating her clothes with newspapers and saving empty containers. The nieces grow in opposite directions, with one leaving to pursue a "normal" life and the other so drawn to her aunt's ways that the two eventually leave to hop a train together.

Housing Court

Type: 16mm film, video
Length: 30 min.
Cost: Purchase $425 (film), $295 (video); rental $55
Source: The Cinema Guild
               1697 Broadway
               New York, NY 10019
               (212) 246-5522
Date: 1985

The Bronx Housing Court in New York City is the setting for examining three buildings where tenants have sought relief in disputes with landlords. The court is viewed as the stage on which the crisis in affordable, decent housing is played out in 125,000 cases annually, dealing with evictions, code violations, and rent strikes.

In the Wee Wee Hours

Type: 16mm film, video
Length: 20 min.
Cost: Purchase $550 (film), $375 (¾"); rental $75 (VHS)
Source: Izak Ben-meir
               307 Marine Street, Apt. C
               Santa Monica, CA 90405
               (213) 399-1996
Date: 1987

Los Angeles's Skid Row by night is the setting for this Oscar-nominated film, which is narrated by a decorated former fighter pilot and POW who became homeless.

Ironweed

Type:	Video
Length:	135 min.
Cost:	Home video rental
Source:	Local video stores
Date:	1987

Though not about homelessness in the 1980s, this film depicts the pain of that life in graphic terms. Based on William Kennedy's novel about Depression-era Albany, the story follows Jack Phelan, an alcoholic who has left his family and is subsisting on the street with Helen Archer, also an alcoholic, played by Meryl Streep. As they scrounge for money for booze and places to sleep, witness the exposure death of a friend, and struggle with their pasts, they depict some of the enduring aspects of being homeless.

Locked Out of the American Dream

Type:	Video
Length:	60 min.
Source:	KERA-TV 3000
	Harry Hines Boulevard
	Dallas, TX 75201
	(214) 871-1390
Date:	1988

This examination of the growing shortage of affordable housing focuses on one Dallas family as it discusses the history of federal involvement in assisted housing for the poor. Profiles are offered of Boston and Baltimore, where nonprofit organizations have joined with developers and public agencies to create affordable housing. Developer James Rouse of Columbia, Maryland, and Boston's Mayor Raymond Flynn are interviewed.

The Many Faces of Homelessness

Type:	Video
Length:	35 min.
Cost:	Purchase $19.95 ($\frac{1}{2}''$), $49.95 ($\frac{3}{4}''$)
Source:	Home Builders Institute
	Fifteenth and M Streets, NW
	Washington, DC 20005
	(800) 368-5242
Date:	1988

The homebuilders' industry prepared this film for its first industry event on homelessness. The film examines daily life for the homeless as well as the builder's role in solving all aspects of the problem, from shelter to permanent housing.

No Home on the Island
Type: 16mm film, video
Length: 29 min.
Cost: Purchase $525 (film), $300 (video); rental $55
Source: Filmakers Library
             124 East Fortieth Street
             New York, NY 10016
             (212) 808-4980
Date: 1987

Homelessness on city streets is familiar to many Americans. Not so readily does the nation come to grips with homelessness in suburban areas. This film, directed by Mark Gross, shows a Long Island community where average, middle-class people experience the need for shelter when faced with job loss, social services cutbacks, recession, and escalating housing costs. Volunteer efforts to help those in need are spotlighted.

Poverty
Type: 16mm film, video
Length: 18 min.
Cost: Purchase $350 (film), $200 (video); rental $50
Source: The Cinema Guild
             1697 Broadway
             New York, NY 10019
             (212) 246-5522
Date: 1976

The late Michael Harrington, author of many works on poverty including *The Other America* and *The New Poverty,* comments on the continuing U.S. problem of a growing gap between the nation's rich and poor.

Promises To Keep
Type: 16mm film, video
Length: 57 min.
Cost: Purchase $250 ($200 for nonprofits); rental $100
Source: Durrin Productions
             1748 Kalorama Road, NW
             Washington, DC 20009
             (202) 387-6700
Date: 1989

Directed by Ginny Durrin, this Oscar-nominated documentary tells the story of the four-year struggle by Mitch Snyder and the Washington,

D.C.–based Community for Creative Non-Violence to hold onto a previously abandoned federal building they have converted into an emergency shelter. Through film clips, press reports, and the words of the homeless themselves, the successful fight to secure the building as a model facility is shown. A discussion guide is available.

Samaritan: The Mitch Snyder Story

Type:	Video
Length:	104 min.
Cost:	Home video rental
Source:	Local video stores
Date:	1986

Martin Sheen stars as Mitch Snyder in this made-for-television film that was produced following the successful struggle to secure a federal building to shelter the homeless in Washington, D.C. True stories of several homeless people are included as part of the effort to tell the story of the Community for Creative Non-Violence.

Shelter

Type:	Video
Length:	55 min.
Cost:	Purchase $445, rental $75
Source:	Filmakers Library
	124 East Fortieth Street
	New York, NY 10016
	(212) 808-4980
Date:	1986

This film uses interviews and portraits to show the variety of people who become homeless: the longtime jobless, former mental patients, families searching for work. Ideas on how to address the problem and who should bear the cost are shared by government officials, policymakers, and social service providers.

Squatters: The Other Philadelphia Story

Type:	16mm film, video
Length:	27 min.
Cost:	Purchase $425 (film), $300 (video); rental $50
Source:	The Cinema Guild
	1697 Broadway
	New York, NY 10019
	(212) 246-5522
Date:	1984

This story of squatters reclaiming buildings in Philadelphia traces not only their need for housing, but also their personal and political transformation as they lobby officials, testify in Congress, and raise funds for their cause.

Streetwise
Type: Video
Length: 92 min.
Cost: Home video rental
Source: Local video stores
Date: 1985

This film examines the pain and courage of homeless teenagers on the streets of Seattle, watching closely as they survive by forming their own community and supporting themselves through panhandling, dealing drugs, and working as prostitutes. Martin Bell directed this story, which was nominated for an Academy Award for Best Documentary in 1984.

Photographic and Other Exhibits

Homeless in America: A Photographic Project
Source: National Mental Health Association
1021 Prince Street
Alexandria, VA 22314
(703) 684-7722

Families for the Homeless, a nonpartisan partnership of congressional, administration, and media families, joined with the National Mental Health Association to create this major traveling photography exhibit on homelessness. Some of the nation's most prominent photojournalists participated in the project, which was funded by public and private sponsors. The exhibit, composed of about 70 framed photos plus text and title panels, is available to museums across the country. An accompanying book and a video are also available.

Portraits of the Powerless
Source: Jim Hubbard, photographer
8104 Chester
Takoma Park, MD 20912
(202) 265-9592

This photography exhibit created by Jim Hubbard was first shown at the American Institute of Architects symposium on shelter. The black-and-white show has been exhibited around the country and is available for community organizations and other groups to display locally.

Search for Shelter Exhibit

Source: American Institute of Architects
                   1735 New York Avenue, NW
                   Washington, DC 20006
                   (202) 626-7468

Twenty-four of the original 37 communities to undertake Search for
Shelter projects now have construction underway; this exhibit chronicles
the original designs and the progress in each community. The exhibit
consists of 26 framed panels, each 20″ × 30″, suitable for wall mounting.
The exhibit is circulated for the cost of expenses.

Shooting Back

Source: Shooting Back
                   c/o Jim Hubbard
                   8104 Chester
                   Takoma Park, MD 20912
                   (202) 265-9592

This model photography program was organized by Jim Hubbard to
engage professional photographers in a learning and teaching experience
with homeless children in the Washington, D.C., shelters. Volunteer photographers from prestigious national media outlets visit the welfare hotels
and shelters to help as children learn the basics of handling a camera and
endeavor to capture the reality of their own lives on film. The children's
work is scheduled for a gallery show in Washington, D.C., in 1990.

Glossary

affordable The U.S. Department of Housing and Urban Development (HUD) considers housing affordable for low-income people if it costs no more than 30 percent of the household's income. Prior to 1981, the standard was 25 percent of adjusted household income.

Aid to Families with Dependent Children (AFDC) A federal assistance program enacted in 1962 that is an extension of the 1935 Social Security Act provision called Aid to Dependent Children (ADC). For a family to receive an AFDC cash assistance payment, the family's income must fall below a certain fixed standard and children must be in need of support because one of their parents has died, is disabled, is not in the home, or is unemployed. AFDC benefit payments are determined by how many people are in the household and by any other income or assets available. Each state sets its standard of need and payment levels, and then matches federal payments on a 50-50 basis. Each state includes shelter in its standard of need; some states make an explicit shelter payment. AFDC recipients may be eligible to receive Medicaid and food stamps as well.

Callahan consent decree Court settlement to the *Callahan v. Carey* lawsuit filed in New York City in 1979 that guaranteed a right to shelter for homeless men. The agreement signed to conclude the case spelled out the men's right and the standards to be met by the city in providing shelter.

chronically mentally ill A state of severe and persistent mental disorder (e.g., schizophrenia or depression) that interferes with function and requires long-term psychiatric care.

commodities Surplus agricultural products that are purchased under the Price Support Program by the federal government and distributed by way of two basic outlets: through mass meal programs, including school lunch programs, large soup kitchens, and other congregate feeding sites, and through food banks and social service programs that provide food packages to individuals and families.

Comprehensive Homeless Assistance Plan (CHAP) A document required of all cities, counties, and states eligible for McKinney programs funds. CHAPs must describe need; inventory existing facilities and services; provide a strategy for matching needs with services; account for the needs of targeted groups; including homeless families with children, the elderly, the mentally ill, and veterans; and explain how federal funds will aid these efforts.

day labor Usually manual labor jobs available to homeless and poor workers on a temporary basis. Job seekers wait on designated street corners or appear at a for-profit labor center in hopes of being assigned to a job, such as loading trucks or cleaning out abandoned buildings. Workers are paid low wages, charged for the necessities of their job (such as rides, shovels, gloves), and are not protected from unsafe conditions or unfair practices.

deinstitutionalization Officially defined by the National Institute of Mental Health as the prevention of inappropriate mental hospital admissions through the provision of community alternatives for treatment, the release to the community of all institutionalized patients who have been given adequate preparation for such discharge, and the establishment and maintenance of community support systems for noninstitutionalized people receiving mental health services in the community.

doubling-up An accommodation to the housing crisis in which one household shares its housing with at least one other household, related or unrelated. This is frequently found among the poor and the breakdown of such arrangements is a leading cause of homelessness.

Emergency Assistance to Families (EAF) A short-term federal emergency aid entitlement program under which states elect to participate in a 50–50 match to provide services, including temporary shelter, for needy families. Twenty-eight states are enrolled.

expiring subsidies Under the Section 8 certificate program, private owners have contracted with the federal government so that owners reserve their housing units for low- and moderate-income people in exchange for a guaranteed long-term rent. When these contracts expire the subsidies are lost, and owners can elect to charge a higher rent or convert the building to another use. Some 700,000 units are jeopardized by this circumstance over the next five years.

fair market rent A cost assigned by the U.S. Department of Housing and Urban Development (HUD) to a typical rental unit in a given geographic area for households of differing sizes. Fair market rents are used to calculate payments for low-income tenants using assisted housing programs, in which HUD will pay the difference between 30 percent of a person's income and the fair market rent.

flops or flop houses   Hotels in which rooms generally are cheaply rented by the night. Usually only a bed is provided, and it is often in a space just big enough to accommodate it.

food bank   A nonprofit clearinghouse for surplus or salvaged food. Producers, markets, and food outlets such as restaurants can donate food, which can then be stored, if necessary, and redistributed to soup kitchens, shelters, and social service agencies. Food banks generally charge a nominal fee to recipients (such as ten cents a pound) to cover operations.

food stamps   In 1961, the U.S. Department of Agriculture (USDA) enacted the food stamp program, technically known as the Family Nutrition Program. It extends to all 50 states and is administered by welfare or social service departments. The USDA pays the full value of the stamps and half the administrative costs. Free stamps are made available to families without the cash to purchase them; a family's allotment is determined by subtracting 30 percent of its monthly income from the Thrifty Food Plan cost for a family of that size. The balance is given to the family in free stamps.

general assistance (GA)   State and local welfare programs for people who do not qualify for federal benefits are typically called general assistance, general relief, home relief, or public assistance. These programs offer income supports to needy people who meet financial eligibility rules. GA programs exist in about two-thirds of the states, although only very short-term aid or one-time aid is available in some of these. Some programs restrict coverage to "temporarily disabled" persons who are awaiting Supplemental Security Income (SSI) coverage. Some programs offer a specific shelter payment; others pay consolidated benefits.

gentrification   The purposeful transformation of a neighborhood into an area that will attract higher-income residents through the displacement of lower-income tenants, the renovation of vacant buildings, and the opening of higher-price businesses.

Good Samaritan laws   Also known as donor liability laws, these statutes enacted by virtually all the states protect food donors. The laws provide that excess food donated to food banks, soup kitchens, or similar outlets is given in good faith with regard to its condition and that the donor is not responsible after the act of giving.

Greyhound therapy   The often officially sanctioned practice of providing one-way bus tickets to homeless persons or others seeking shelter or benefits if the applicant cannot prove local ties or is deemed otherwise undesirable in the local community. It is a practice also used to move newly discharged mental patients or just-released prisoners to different communities.

housing trust fund A revenue pool for the creation of low- and moderate-income housing. Trust funds are created by state legislation or voter initiative and generally are fueled by real estate–related revenues, either developers' contributions, taxes, fees, or grants.

in rem **housing** Residential property taken by a local jurisdiction in a tax foreclosure proceeding. These units often cannot be reoccupied because local governments do not have the funds to rehabilitate them after seizure.

inclusionary zoning A requirement for developers to include affordable housing in exchange for certain development rights or bonus allowances.

linkage A development requirement under which for-profit building at one location is related to development at another site involving low- or moderate-income housing.

low income The U.S. Department of Housing and Urban Development defines low-income people as those whose household income is between 50 and 80 percent of the area median income, adjusted for household size; very low income is defined as below 50 percent.

McKinney Act Any of a number of programs under the most significant piece of federal legislation to address homelessness, the Stewart B. McKinney Homeless Assistance Act, first passed in 1987 as PL 100-77. The act is named for the late Representative Stewart B. McKinney (R-CT), a member of the Housing Subcommittee who was concerned about the problems of the homeless.

magnet theory The idea, proposed by public officials or residents who are opposed to measures that assist the homeless in their community, that the availability of such assistance will attract homeless people from other areas.

NIMBY an abbreviation for "not in my backyard," which refers to people in residential areas resisting the siting of any facility perceived as undesirable and affecting neighborhood quality and property values. The term includes, but is not limited to, the presence of shelters, drug treatment facilities, community residences for the mentally ill, halfway houses, sewage treatment plants, jails, and toxic waste facilities.

overcrowding The U.S. Department of Housing and Urban Development classifies a housing unit as overcrowded if more than one person per room is housed there.

prepayment   Owners of buildings who used federal mortgage subsidies to develop projects where some or all of the units were rented to low- or moderate-income persons for a period of 20 years may elect to end their obligation to the subsidy program by paying off the mortgage before its due date. This jeopardizes the tenancy of the lower-income people, who may be forced to seek other housing if the use of the building is changed.

poverty line   An official measure of the income needed to provide basic necessities. The 1985 poverty line for a family of three was $8,573.

Section 8   A U.S. Department of Housing and Urban Development program that provides low-income housing by giving certificates or vouchers to low-income people to help pay for existing housing.

single room occupancy (SRO)   SRO dwellings are inexpensive rental living accommodations, often in a hotel setting. Residents have private rooms but share bathrooms and kitchen space, if available. SROs are usually found in older downtown areas; hundreds of thousands of such affordable units were destroyed during the past decade of redevelopment projects. Some nonprofit organizations have begun to develop SRO projects, and some units are also funded by the McKinney Act.

skid row   The traditional name given to downtown areas where the homeless people of earlier decades could be found. The name supposedly originated in Seattle, from the road where logs were "skidded" to the waterfront. Such areas have been wiped out by development in many cities, taking with them the marginal commercial enterprises and cheap housing that were supported by their low-income residents.

soup kitchen   Typically places where one or more meals are served on a regular schedule, generally at no cost to the recipients. Many soup kitchens are in churches, shelters, or other community facilities; they are usually staffed by volunteers who procure food from donations and food banks.

substandard   Housing is considered substandard by the U.S. Department of Housing and Urban Development and the Bureau of the Census if it has certain physical or structural deficiencies, such as an absence of plumbing or heating equipment, holes in the walls, or rats or mice.

Supplemental Security Income (SSI)   A federal benefit program, authorized under the Social Security Act and begun in 1974, that makes cash payments to the aged, blind, and disabled. Eligibility is determined on the basis of need, using nationwide standards based on the poverty threshold and related to the consumer price index with the same formula used for Social Security benefits. Non-recipients of Social Security can receive SSI if they qualify.

transitional housing A second stage of shelter for homeless people, usually smaller in scale than emergency facilities but often a multifamily residence. Residents generally stay in transitional programs for flexible but not indefinite periods of up to two years, with supportive services available to prepare them for greater self-sufficiency and independent living. Such services include counseling, job training, parenting classes, and budgeting.

vouchers A federal housing assistance program for in which the government pays the difference between 30 percent of a tenant's income and a "payment standard" for a unit selected by the tenant. Unlike Section 8 certificates, vouchers may be used where tenants have selected units at any rent level, not just at fair market rent.

warehousing (1) The practice of keeping habitable dwelling units off the rental market in order to have enough vacant units in a building to meet legal requirements for selling it or converting it to a condominium or cooperative. (2) The practice of providing emergency shelter in minimal surroundings, generally in a mass shelter where the homeless are offered little besides a cot or mat for the night.

welfare hotels Commercially owned hotels or motels used to provide shelter to homeless families, generally those on public assistance. Physical conditions and services are often inadequate; cooking facilities are generally not provided.

Index